D1491300

T · H · E

SICILIAN-
AMERICAN

COOKBOOK

T · H · E

SICILIAN-AMERICAN

COOKBOOK

Continental Cuisine
for the Health Conscious American

Santo and Mabel Formica

August House / Little Rock
PUBLISHERS

Printed in the United States of America

10 9 8 7 6 5 4 3 2 1

LIBRARY OF CONGRESS
CATALOGING-IN-PUBLICATION DATA
Formica, Santo D.
The Sicilian-American cookbook:
continental cuisine for the health-conscious American/
Santo and Mabel Formica.—1st ed. p. cm.
ISBN 0-87483-114-8 (alk. paper): $13.95
1. Cookery, Italian-Sicilian style. 2. Cookery, American.
I. Formica, Mabel. II. Title.
TX723.2.S55F67 1990
641.5945'8—dc20   90-224
CIP

First Edition, 1990

Cover design by Wendell E. Hall
Typography by Lettergraphics, Little Rock, Arkansas
Design direction by Communication Graphics
Project direction by Suzanne Rogers
Woodcut illustrations by John Deering
Wine consulting by Wallace A. Geiringer, Jr.

This book is printed on archival-quality paper which meets the
guidelines for performance and durability of the Committee on
Production Guidelines for Book Longevity of the Council on
Library Resources.

AUGUST HOUSE, INC.   PUBLISHERS   LITTLE ROCK

To our children

Connie, Ross, Vicki, Becca and Sandi

*who survived the trials
and tribulations of being our "taste panel" for
many of the new recipes.*

CONTENTS

INTRODUCTION

All the recipes originated in our kitchen and were designed for ease of preparation and to promote the consumption of poultry. The per capita consumption of chicken and turkey has dramatically increased in the past thirty years. Why? Poultry is low in calories, high in quality protein, has many health benefits and is the lowest cost meat available today. Many fish recipes are also included since fish and poultry go hand in hand in providing health benefits and a delicious meal.

The Sicilian recipes have been handed down orally from family members and are recorded here for the first time; we hope you enjoy. Note that many of the dishes are meatless, but not by choice. The Sicilian farmer-peasant could not afford meat everyday. Cheese, fish and legumes were the main source of protein. Meat was eaten with relish on Sunday, feast days and special occasions. The mainstays for hardworking Sicilians were pasta, fresh vegetables, fruits, nuts and wine. Wine was consumed at each meal in the same manner we drink coffee, milk or iced tea.

The Sicilians copied the Moor practice of finishing their meals with expresso. When trading and negotiating for goods, the Moors would wine and dine the Sicilians late into the night, drinking lots of expresso. They were alert, but the Sicilians were half asleep and ended up on the short end of the trading stick. It didn't take the Sicilians long to realize the benefits of expresso. With the two sides fully alert, the Sicilians quickly got the upper hand and the best of the barter sessions. We must admit, the Moors may contest that conclusion.

Sicilian cooking was influenced by the Phoenicians, the Greeks and North Africans. This may account for the large diversity in Sicilian food preparation; even in a small island area very definite cooking styles exist. For example, around Marsala tomato sauce is seasoned with sweet anise; up the coast from Palermo, they add sugar to their sauce; near and around Messina, you would be reported to the *capo* if you added the above ingredients to a pasta sauce.

Even though a Roman wrote the first cookbook, *The Art of Cooking by Apicius,* in the first century A.D., it was the Sicilians who put the cooking of the Mediterranean basin together and made it a distinct cuisine. Recently, a series of tablets displaying recipes were found in Iraq which date from the time between 1100 and 700 B.C.—before Apicius. We still believe an Italian wrote the first complete cookbook.

Sicilian cooking is based on fresh fruits, vegetables and herbs. If available, fresh basil, oregano, parsley and garlic make a world of difference in tomato sauces.

The grade of olive oil used is very important; there are three:
Extra virgin (the first pressing)—low in acid, distinctive greenish color, odor and taste. A must for salad and vegetable dishes.

Virgin (the second pressing)—higher level of acid not meeting specifications of extra virgin olive oil. The odor and taste are milder. Best for salads and vegetables.

Pure olive oil—this means it contains 100 % olive oil and nothing else. It is higher in acid and the color varies. The taste and odor are very mild. It is used mostly for cooking and basting sauces.

To tell which olive oil you like, buy a small quantity and put it in a wine glass. Smell, look at the color and taste.

Buy olive oil in quantities that can be used in 4 to 6 weeks. Keep it in the refrigerator for a longer shelf life.

Use fresh herbs whenever available. Go to your farmer's market and pick up several plants of basil and oregano. They grow well in flower pots. Fresh parsley is always available in the curly variety, but the Italian single leaf variety is preferred. It has more flavor and you can grow it from seed.

About Dry Wines
When a crisp, dry Italian white wine is recommended, don't hesitate to try a recent vintage (1 or 2 years old) white from a reliable producer—Bolla, Anselmi, Antinori, Lungarotti, Boscaini. The key is young freshness of the vintage. A 3 year old vintage is too old. In contrast, a good red wine should be 4 to 5 years old.

Note
Occasionally, recipes will include references to other recipes listed in the book. Those entries are featured in bold italic and can be located in the index.

Appetizers

Artichoke Dip

2 14½-ounce cans artichoke hearts, chopped fine
1 cup Parmesan or Romano cheese
1 cup mayonnaise
1 teaspoon garlic powder or 3 cloves garlic, minced
1 teaspoon curry powder

Preheat oven to 350°. Blend all ingredients in a mixing bowl. Pour into pan and bake 30 minutes. Cool and sprinkle with additional curry powder. Serve with crackers or rye bread squares.

Yields 15 to 20 servings.

Wine selection: Corvo Bianco, a Sicilian smooth dry white

Stuffed Artichokes

4 large artichokes, washed and drained with tough outer leaves and stem removed
olive oil, extra virgin or pure

Breading:
⅔ cup dry bread crumbs
⅓ cup Parmesan cheese, grated
1 teaspoon garlic powder
½ teaspoon black pepper
2 tablespoons parsley, chopped coarse

Blend all ingredients. With your fingers, spread leaves on artichokes. Generously dribble breading between each leaf and in the middle. Dribble 1 teaspoon olive oil over each artichoke after stuffing. Place artichokes standing up in a 6-quart pan with 1 inch of water. Bring to a boil, reduce heat, cover and simmer 1 hour (add water if necessary) or until a leaf can be pulled out easily. Serve at room temperature.

Wine selection: Asti Spumanti, sweet and sparkling

Garlic Bread Ricotta

6 large kaiser rolls, each half cut in 6 pieces
3/4 cup extra virgin olive oil
4 large cloves garlic, crushed in a heavy skillet
1 cup ricotta cheese
1 cup black olives, sliced
black pepper

Pour olive oil in skillet with crushed garlic and sauté 1 to 2 minutes (garlic should turn light brown). Remove from heat; discard garlic. Brush each piece of bread with oil and toast in a preheated broiler until golden brown. Immediately dot with 3/4 teaspoon ricotta in 5 or 6 places. Sprinkle lightly with pepper. Top with sliced olives and serve warm or at room temperature.

Yields 12 to 36 servings.

Wine selection: Anselmi Soave, a crisp dry white

Sautéed Calamari Smothered

2 pounds squid, cleaned and cut in 1-inch pieces with tentacles left intact
3 cloves garlic, minced fine
1/4 cup olive oil, extra virgin or pure
1 heaping teaspoon parsley, chopped
1/4 cup red wine vinegar

Sauté garlic in olive oil in a 10-inch skillet with a tight cover over medium-high heat 1 minute. Add squid and sauté 5 to 6 minutes, add parsley and toss, then add vinegar and quickly cover. Lower heat and cook 4 minutes. Remove from stove and let cool, covered, about 30 minutes. Place in a bowl and serve at room temperature or chilled. Makes an unusual appetizer.

Sicilian Camponata

½ cup olive oil, extra virgin or pure
3 pounds tomatoes, blanched, peeled and chopped coarse
3 pounds eggplant, peeled and cubed in ½-inch chunks
2 bell peppers, seeded and cut in ½-inch chunks
5 large cloves garlic, minced coarse
2 medium-large yellow onions, cut in half and sliced thin
1 cup celery, cut in ½-inch chunks with leaves included
½ cup red wine vinegar
½ cup fresh parsley, chopped coarse
⅓ cup fresh basil, chopped coarse
¾ cup salad green olives, chopped coarse
½ cup pine nuts or chopped walnuts
3 slender carrots, sliced thin
2 slender zucchini, sliced thin
1 6-ounce can tomato paste
2 tablespoons salt
2 tablespoons sugar
1 tablespoon black pepper

Place cubed eggplant on paper towels. Sprinkle lightly with salt and let stand at least 1 hour; pat dry. Prepare all other ingredients as instructed. Over medium-high heat, place olive oil in 8- to 10-quart pot and lightly brown pine nuts 1 to 2 minutes; remove with slotted spoon. Brown eggplant lightly, about 7 to 8 minutes. Add all ingredients and stir slowly, blending everything. Bring to a boil; reduce heat and simmer covered 30 minutes exactly.

Meanwhile, sterilize 8 pint jars, lids and caps. Fill solid and let cool overnight. Refrigerate. Will keep 4 months. Serve as an appetizer on crackers or with Italian bread. The key to delicious camponata is the use of fresh grown ingredients and fully ripe tomatoes. Bon Appetito!

Wine selection: Ricosoli Chianti, a fruity, medium-bodied dry red

Joe C. Camponata II

2 large eggplants, unpeeled and cut in 1-inch cubes
2 large white or yellow onions, cut in ½-inch pieces
2 or 3 sticks celery, cut in ¼-inch pieces
8 or 10 cloves garlic, chopped medium
½ to 1 cup olive oil or more
3 or 4 plum tomatoes, cut in ½-inch pieces or smaller
10 to 15 pitted green Sicilian or Spanish olives, slivered
salt and pepper
1 or 2 tablespoons red pepper flakes or to taste
1 or 2 tablespoons parsley, chopped
1-pound can Italian plum tomatoes , cut in 1-inch pieces or smaller
1 6-ounce can tomato paste
5 or 6 anchovy fillets, mashed with fork with oil added
2 or 3 tablespoons sugar
½ to ¾ cup red wine vinegar
6 to 8 tablespoons large imported capers
6 to 8 tablespoons pinolis (pine nuts)
water as needed

Sauté eggplant, onion, celery and garlic in olive oil. Salt and pepper to taste. Continue until tender and starts to brown. Remove and put aside. In same oil, sauté fresh tomatoes and olives about 15 minutes or until tomatoes begin to soften. Transfer to a large pot and add eggplant mixture and all other ingredients while simmering over medium heat. Stir frequently to avoid sticking to bottom of pan. Simmer about 30 minutes. Add water if mixture becomes too dry. Cover and chill well before serving. Serve on slices of fresh Italian bread, crackers or lettuce leaves with bread sticks. Garnish with wedge of lemon.

Chicken Livers Genoa Style

1 pound fresh chicken livers, cleaned and cut in quarters
1 cup flour, seasoned to taste
¹/₄ cup pure olive oil
1 teaspoon dried oregano
³/₄ teaspoon dried basil or 1 tablespoon fresh basil
¹/₄ cup wine vinegar
garlic powder to taste

Place livers in a paper bag with flour and shake until evenly coated; brush off excess. In a heavy skillet over medium-high heat, sauté livers in oil 5 minutes or until lightly brown (sprinkle garlic powder, basil and oregano over livers as you are browning them). Stir livers quickly, add wine and vinegar and cover tightly; cook 2 minutes. Let stand 2 minutes and serve hot.

Yields 10 to 12 servings.

Chicken Livers in Wine Sauce

1 pound chicken livers
¹/₄ cup cooking oil
¹/₂ cup flour
¹/₂ teaspoon pepper
³/₄ teaspoon salt
¹/₂ teaspoon garlic powder
¹/₂ cup dry white wine
1 tablespoon Worcestershire sauce
Accent (MSG)

Wash livers and drain; sprinkle with Accent. In a medium-size paper bag, thoroughly mix the salt, pepper and flour. Put livers in the paper bag and shake until well coated. Brown livers individually in a heavy skillet. Mix the wine and Worcestershire sauce, return livers to skillet, pour the wine mixture over them and cover tightly; simmer 10 minutes. To serve, cut the livers into bite-size pieces and place on a chafing dish.

Chicken Meatballs

1 pound ground chicken
2 slices day old bread, soaked in water (squeeze out excess water)
1 egg, slightly beaten
1 large clove garlic, finely minced
2 tablespoons parsley, finely minced
1 teaspoon pepper
1 teaspoon salt
1 teaspoon mustard

Combine all ingredients and blend thoroughly. Form into marble-size balls and brown quickly in hot oil. Cook in your favorite tomato sauce ¹/₂ hour and serve hot.

Yields 30 meatballs.

Chicken Nuggets in Wine

1 pound chicken breasts, cut into nuggets
1 pound boneless, skinless thigh meat, cut into nuggets
salt and pepper to taste
¹/₂ cup pure olive oil
2 cloves garlic, minced
¹/₂ cup dry white wine
2 tablespoons pure olive oil
¹/₂ teaspoon rosemary, crushed
1 tablespoon parsley, chopped coarse

Season nuggets and set aside. In a medium bowl, mix ¹/₂ cup olive oil and garlic. Add nuggets and stir until well coated. In a skillet over medium-high heat, add 2 tablespoons olive oil; sauté nuggets until lightly browned (about 3 to 4 minutes). Sprinkle with rosemary and parsley and stir. Add wine and blend; cook 3 to 4 minutes. Serve hot or at room temperature with toothpicks.

Yields 18 to 20 servings.

Wine selection: Barbera

Chicken Party Morsels

1 pound chicken breasts, cut into nuggets
salt and pepper to taste
Pam

Breading:

²/₃ cup dry bread crumbs
¹/₃ cup Parmesan cheese, grated
1 teaspoon garlic powder
2 tablespoons parsley, chopped coarse

Dip nuggets in olive oil; coat with bread crumb mix. Place each piece on a toothpick and place on a broiler sprayed with Pam. Cook 4 minutes or until brown.

Yields 20 servings.

Pick-Up Chicken Sticks

3 pounds chicken wings
1 cup butter
1¹/₂ cups flour, sifted
¹/₃ cup sesame seeds
1 teaspoon salt
¹/₂ teaspoon pepper
¹/₂ teaspoon oregano
1 teaspoon Accent (MSG)

Cut off and discard tips of chicken wings. Divide each wing in half by cutting through the joint with a sharp knife. Wash and drain. Melt butter in large, shallow baking pan. Mix flour, salt, pepper, sesame seed, oregano and Accent in a pie pan. One at a time, roll chicken pieces in butter, letting any excess drip off. Coat generously in flour mixture and set aside on sheets of waxed paper. Arrange, not touching, in a single layer in pan. Bake at 350° 40 minutes or until tender and golden on the bottom. Slide pan into heated broiler 3 to 5 minutes or until tops are brown.

Pollettini Cocktail Treats

2 pounds boned chicken (include breasts, legs, thighs and skin), ground
2 slices day old bread, soaked in water (squeeze out excess)
2 eggs, slightly beaten
2 large cloves garlic, finely minced
2 rounded tablespoons parsley, finely minced
2 rounded teaspoons Accent (MSG)
1 teaspoon pepper
1 1/2 teaspoons salt
1 teaspoon dry mustard

Combine all ingredients and blend thoroughly. Form into large marble-size balls and brown quickly in hot oil. Cook in your favorite tomato sauce 1/2 hour and serve hot as an appetizer. Yields 50.

Polloburgers

1 pound chicken, ground
1/3 pound pork shoulder, ground
3/4 teaspoon pepper
1 teaspoon salt
1 clove garlic, minced
1 small onion, minced

Combine all ingredients and blend thoroughly. Form into patties and fry or broil. Cut into bite-size pieces and serve.

Crab and Clam Appetizer

1 6½-ounce can crab meat and juice
1 6½-ounce can minced clams and juice
3 cloves garlic, minced
1 cup Parmesan cheese, grated
juice of 1 lemon
1 tablespoon Worcestershire sauce
⅓ cup extra virgin olive oil
⅓ cup parsley, chopped coarse
½ cup sweet red onion, chopped fine
2 teaspoons Dijon mustard
1 teaspoon pepper

Sauté garlic in preheated olive oil 30 seconds and remove from heat. In a mixing bowl, combine remaining ingredients. Add oil and garlic. Toss and mix until well blended. Chill several hours or overnight. Serve on party rye or crackers.

Yields enough spread for 30 servings.

Wine selection: Rhine or Saturne, very flavorful sweet or dry white

Sicilian Bagno Freddo and Caldo

Italian Dips for Veggies

Freddo (Cold)

3/4 cup extra virgin olive oil
1/4 cup red wine vinegar
1 2-ounce can anchovy
3 cloves garlic, cut in half
1 tablespoon Dijon mustard
2 tablespoons fresh lemon juice
1/2 teaspoon flaked red pepper (optional)

Place all ingredients in a blender and mix at medium speed 2 minutes, then at high speed 1 minute. Serve with an assortment of vegetables cut up for dipping.

Caldo (Warm)

1 cup heavy cream
1 cup extra virgin olive oil
3 cloves garlic, minced
1 2-ounce can anchovy, minced
1 tablespoon Worcestershire sauce

Heat oil in a heavy skillet. Add garlic and sauté 30 seconds. Add anchovy, stir, reduce heat, and slowly add cream, stirring all the time. Cook about 5 minutes. Transfer to a warming dish and keep warm with a candle. Serve with an assortment of vegetables for dipping. Goes well for dipping bread sticks and cooked artichoke leaves.

Both dips yield 10 to 12 servings.

Elegant Eggplant Spread

1 1/2-pound eggplant, peeled and cut in 1-inch cubes
salt and pepper to taste
3 cloves garlic, cut in half
1/3 cup fresh parsley, no stems
1/4 cup fresh basil, no stems or 1 1/3 teaspoons dry
1/4 cup pine nuts or walnuts
3 tablespoons extra virgin olive oil
2 tablespoons fresh lemon juice
1 large tomato, diced fine

Sprinkle eggplant with salt and let stand 30 minutes; boil in salted water 8 minutes. Drain in colander and cool on paper towels. Blend eggplant and remaining ingredients, except tomato, 2 minutes on medium setting. Pour into dish and stir in tomato. Serve chilled with rye bread or crackers.

Yields 15 to 20 servings.

Wine selection: Frascati

Marinated Eggplant

2 pounds eggplant, peeled and sliced 1/2-inch thick and cut in 1-inch pieces
2 cups mushrooms, sliced

Basic Marinade:

1/2 cup olive oil, extra virgin or pure
1/2 cup red wine vinegar
juice of 1 lemon
1 teaspoon salt
1 teaspoon black pepper
3/4 teaspoon flaked red pepper
1 1/2 tablespoons dry oregano
5 large cloves garlic, finely minced

Lightly salt eggplant and drain on paper towels 30 minutes; pat dry. In a 6-quart saucepan, add eggplant to boiling water. Reduce heat and simmer uncovered no longer than 8 minutes. Drain in a colander until cool enough to handle; drain on paper towels and pat dry. In a large mixing bowl, combine all ingredients for marinade and blend. Add mushrooms and eggplant and toss gently. Cover and let stand at room temperature 4 hours; toss several times. Refrigerate 1 hour. Serve chilled.

Basic Marinade—Plus

2½ pounds mushrooms, sliced and sautéed in olive oil 4 to 5 minutes
1¼ pounds each of cauliflower and broccoli florets
2½ pounds sweet banana peppers, sliced in ¼-inch rounds and sautéed in olive oil 6 to
    7 minutes
any fresh vegetable
1 pound pasta, cooked al dente

Follow directions for Marinated Eggplant.

Stuffed Eggplant

2 medium eggplants, peeled and cut in scant ¼-inch rounds, soaked in salted water 1 hour
Quickie Twenty Minute Sauce
pure olive oil

Filling:

½ cup mozzarella cheese, shredded
½ cup Parmesan cheese, grated
1 pound ricotta cheese
2 large eggs, beaten
2 tablespoons parsley, chopped coarse
½ teaspoon pepper
1 teaspoon garlic powder

Preheat oven to 350°. Blend ingredients for filling by hand. Remove eggplant slices from water and place on paper towels; pat dry. In a large skillet, cover bottom with ¼-inch olive oil; lightly brown eggplant. Place on paper towels, drain and cool. Place 1 tablespoon filling on each slice of eggplant and roll tightly. Cover bottom of baking pan with some of the Quickie Sauce. Arrange eggplant in rows and cover with remaining sauce. Bake 25 minutes. Makes an excellent warm appetizer.

Yields 10 to 12 servings.

Wine Selection: Cortese di Gavi, a crisp dry white

Deviled Eggs with Chicken Livers

1 pound chicken livers
1/2 cup red onions, finely chopped
1/2 stick butter or margarine
2 dozen large eggs, hard-boiled
1/2 cup sour cream
1/2 cup dry white wine
4 tablespoons prepared mustard
4 tablespoons mayonnaise or salad dressing
1 teaspoon pepper
1 teaspoon salt

Sauté livers in olive oil 8 to 10 minutes; add onions 2 or 3 minutes before livers are cooked. Set aside to cool. Peel eggs and cut in half diagonally. Run the yolks and liver through a blender and place in a large mixing bowl. Add remaining ingredients and blend thoroughly. Stuff each 1/2 egg white generously and sprinkle lightly with paprika. Chill 3 hours before serving.

Genoa Deviled Eggs

12 large eggs, hard-boiled
1 tablespoon *Pesto Sauce*
1/4 cup extra virgin olive oil
1/4 cup sweet red onion, chopped fine
1/4 cup dry white wine
1/2 teaspoon flaked red pepper or to taste
2 tablespoons parsley, minced
salt and pepper to taste

Peel eggs, cut lengthwise and remove yolk. Blend yolks and all ingredients. Adjust seasonings. Fill each half with yolk mixture and garnish with pieces of pimentos.

Yields 24 servings.

Italian Deviled Eggs

12 large eggs, hard-boiled
1 teaspoon garlic powder
$^1/_2$ teaspoon flaked red pepper or to taste
1 medium-ripe tomato, seeded, drained and chopped fine
$^1/_4$ cup sweet red onion, chopped fine
1 tablespoon red wine vinegar
$^1/_2$ stick butter, softened
2 tablespoons fresh parsley, chopped medium
salt and pepper to taste

Peel eggs, cut lengthwise and remove yolk. Combine and blend yolks with all remaining ingredients. Adjust seasonings. Fill each half of egg with yolk mixture and garnish with $^1/_2$ green olive.

Yields 24 servings.

Sicilian Deviled Eggs

12 large eggs, hard-boiled
$6^1/_2$ ounces tuna fish, packed in water, drained
$^1/_4$ cup fresh parsley, chopped fine
2 teaspoons Dijon mustard
$^3/_4$ teaspoon garlic powder
3 tablespoons extra virgin olive oil
12 black olives, cut in half and pitted

Peel eggs, cut in half lengthwise and separate yolks. In a mixing bowl, combine egg yolks, parsley, mustard, garlic powder and olive oil; blend until smooth. Fill each egg white half with mix and garnish with $^1/_2$ black olive. Chill several hours.

Yields 24 servings.

Olives Scaciati

2 pounds Italian or Greek jumbo green olives
2 cups celery (inner stalk), cut in $1/2$-inch pieces, include leaves

Marinade:

$3/4$ cup olive oil, extra virgin or pure
$1/4$ cup red wine vinegar
1 teaspoon black pepper
$3/4$ teaspoon flaked red pepper
2 tablespoons oregano
6 large cloves garlic, chopped medium

Blend marinade thoroughly in a large mixing bowl. Wash olives in cold water and drain, then slightly flatten them with a wooden mallet. Add olives and celery to marinade and toss gently until well coated. Cover and let stand at room temperature 4 to 5 hours or overnight. During this period toss 5 or 6 times; always keep covered. Place olive mix in 2-quart jars, cover and refrigerate. Will keep 2 to 3 months. Serve at room temperature.

Italian Roasted Peppers

6 large meaty bell peppers (3 may be red)
$^1/_3$ cup extra virgin olive oil
1 tablespoon oregano
1 teaspoon dried basil or 3 tablespoons fresh
$^1/_2$ teaspoon flaked red pepper
1 teaspoon salt
$^3/_4$ teaspoon pepper
1 tablespoon sugar

Preheat oven to 400°. Wash and dry peppers; arrange on a cookie sheet and place in middle of oven. Roast 30 to 35 minutes or until brown (turn every 10 to 12 minutes). Remove from oven and immediately place in a heavy brown paper bag. Close bag and roll tightly. Let stand 30 to 40 minutes until cool. Open bag, core peppers and remove seeds and skin. Tear into $^1/_2$-inch strips and place in a medium bowl. Add oil and spices and salt and pepper. Toss gently and coat strips of peppers thoroughly. Serve at room temperature.

Wine selection: Vino Nobile di Montepulciano, a fruity, medium-bodied dry red

Zucchini and Eggs Garden Pyramid

$2^1/_2$- to 3-pounds fresh zucchini, about 2 inches wide and 10 inches long
3 large eggs, hard-boiled
$^1/_4$ cup fresh parsley, chopped medium
$^1/_4$ cup fresh basil, chopped medium or fresh parsley
3 large cloves garlic, chopped fine
$^1/_2$ cup Parmesan or Romano cheese, grated
salt and pepper to taste
$^1/_2$ to $^2/_3$ cup olive oil, extra virgin or pure (add as needed)

Slice eggs thinly and chill. Slice zucchini in $^1/_4$-inch rounds. Salt and pepper to taste. In a heavy skillet, over medium-high heat, add $^1/_2$ cup olive oil and lightly brown zucchini. Drain on paper towels. Arrange 1 layer of zucchini on a 10-inch serving platter and cover with slices from 1 egg; sprinkle with parsley, basil, garlic and cheese. Repeat 3 times, then end with a layer of zucchini covered with all toppings except eggs. Set aside 2 hours at room temperature to blend flavors. To serve, cut like a cake; run 2 toothpicks through each piece. Can be made in advance—refrigerate overnight.

Wine selection: Centine Bianco, a dry white with a touch of spritziness

Zucchini Pyramid II

3 zucchini, 2 inches wide, 8 to 10 inches long
1 cup Parmesan cheese, grated
olive or vegetable oil as needed

Slice zucchini in ¼-inch rounds; sprinkle with seasoned salt. In a large skillet over medium heat, fry zucchini in oil until lightly browned; drain on paper towels. Arrange 1 layer of cooked zucchini on a 10-inch serving plate and sprinkle generously with cheese. Repeat until all zucchini are used. Sprinkle cheese over top and garnish with chopped parsley or fresh basil. Serve with toothpicks.

Yields 16 to 20 servings.

Zucchini Sticks

8 small, slender zucchini, cut lengthwise in quarters
¼ to ½ cup olive oil, extra virgin or pure
Pam

Breading:

⅔ cup dry bread crumbs
⅓ cup Parmesan cheese, grated
1 teaspoon garlic powder
2 tablespoons parsley, chopped coarse

Preheat oven to 375°. Lightly salt and pepper zucchini, dip in olive oil, then coat in breading. Place zucchini in rows on cookie sheet sprayed with Pam. Bake 20 minutes; serve warm.

Yields 10 to 12 servings.

Salads

Italian Salad Dressing

¹/₂ cup extra virgin olive oil
¹/₃ cup red wine vinegar
¹/₃ cup water
¹/₂ teaspoon salt or to taste
¹/₂ teaspoon pepper or to taste
1 rounded teaspoon oregano
1 teaspoon garlic powder

In a 12-ounce bottle or pint jar with cover, combine all ingredients and shake well.

Yields 6 servings.

Mussel Pasta Salad

2 pounds mussels, washed, sand and beard removed
12 ounces Rotini twists
2 medium zucchini, cut in small cubes
1 bunch green onions, cut in 1-inch pieces including tails
1 pound tomatoes, cut in bite-size pieces

Salad Dressing:

$1/2$ cup extra virgin olive oil
3 tablespoons red wine vinegar
1 rounded tablespoon Dijon mustard
$1/4$ teaspoon flaked red pepper or to taste
$1/4$ cup sweet red onion, chopped medium
3 cloves garlic, minced
$1/4$ cup fresh parsley and basil, mixed together and chopped coarse (use all parsley if basil not available)
salt and pepper to taste

Combine all ingredients in a mixing bowl and blend with a wire whisk. In a 4-quart sauce pan with cover, steam mussels in wine and green onions 6 to 7 minutes. Remove with slotted spoon, cool, remove meat and discard shells. Add 2 quarts water to liquid in sauce pan and cook the rotini, drain (reserve liquid) and set aside. In same liquid, boil zucchini 4 minutes, remove with slotted spoon, cool and set aside. In a large serving bowl, combine pasta, zucchini, mussels and tomatoes; toss gently. Add salad dressing and toss until everything is well coated. Serve chilled on romaine lettuce with a light soup and crusty Italian bread.

Yields 6 to 8 servings.

Wine selection: Santori Pino

Sicilian Caesar Salad

2 heads romaine lettuce, drained and torn into 1- to 2-inch pieces
2 large eggs, coddled
1 1/2 cups seasoned croutons
2 cloves garlic, minced
1 clove garlic, cut in half
1/2 cup extra virgin olive oil
1/4 cup wine vinegar
1 tablespoon lemon juice
1 tablespoon Worcestershire sauce
1/2 cup Parmesan cheese
1 2-ounce can anchovies, drained and chopped

Rub the sides of a large wooden salad bowl with garlic. Add romaine lettuce, croutons and salt and pepper to taste; mix. Place all other ingredients in a pint jar, cover and mix vigorously or place in blender for 1 minute at medium speed. Pour over lettuce, toss and serve immediately.

Yields 8 servings.

Sicilian Tomato and Onion Salad

3 large tomatoes
1 medium sweet Italian red onion, sliced thin
1/4 cup extra virgin olive oil
1 tablespoon dried oregano
salt and pepper to taste

Cut tomatoes in bite-size pieces in a serving bowl. Add remaining ingredients and toss lightly. Serve with Italian bread and cold chicken or cold cuts and cheese.

Yields 6 to 8 servings.

Warm Seafood Salad/Romaine Lettuce

1 head romaine lettuce, torn into 1- to 2-inch pieces
1 pound small or medium shrimp, peeled and deveined or 1 pound small scallops or catfish
  nuggets
4 to 6 banana peppers, cut in ¼-inch rounds with seeds discarded
3 cloves garlic, chopped medium
¼ cup fresh parsley, chopped coarse
1 medium sweet red onion, sliced thin
¼ cup olive oil
¼ cup wine vinegar
seasoned salt to taste

Sauté seasoned fish and peppers in olive oil in a heavy skillet. Stir and cook 3 to 4 minutes over medium-high heat. (Catfish nuggets will need an extra 2 to 3 minutes cooking time.) Add garlic and vinegar. Stir and cover. Cook 1 minute and turn off heat. Let stand 1 minute; add parsley and blend. Serve over lettuce leaves. Cover with red onion slices and garnish with parsley.

Yields 6 servings.

Chicken Salad with Artichoke Hearts

1 pound chicken breasts, cut in 2-inch strips
salt and pepper
1 large bell pepper, cut in 2-inch strips
1 bunch green onions, cut in 1-inch pieces, including tops
3 medium carrots, cut in thin strips
1 cup fresh mushrooms, quartered
1 head romaine lettuce, torn into 1-inch pieces, outer leaves discarded
½ cup of your favorite Italian salad dressing
    (for reduced calories substitute ⅛ cup lemon juice)
1 4-ounce jar marinated artichoke hearts, drained and quartered
3 tablespoons extra virgin olive oil
⅓ cup wine vinegar

Salt and pepper chicken strips to taste; place in a heavy skillet and sauté in olive oil 2 to 3 minutes or until lightly browned. Cover tightly a few seconds. Add green peppers, onions and vinegar. Cover quickly and turn off heat; let stand 3 minutes. In a large mixing bowl, combine all the other vegetables and toss. Pour chicken and contents of skillet over greens and mix. Add salad dressing and mix. Serve immediately or refrigerate 1 hour and serve chilled.

Yields 6 servings.

Chicken Bonanza Salad

1 3½- to 4-pound chicken or turkey, cooked and cut into bite-size pieces
2 medium potatoes, boiled, peeled and diced
2 large eggs, hard-boiled and diced
1 medium sweet red onion, diced
1 tablespoon diced green Spanish olive
6 slices of bacon
1 teaspoon leaf oregano
salt and pepper to taste
2 tablespoons vinegar
6 large lettuce leaves

Combine all ingredients in a large bowl, except bacon and lettuce. Salt and pepper to taste. Dice bacon and fry until crisp and let stand 2 minutes. Pour bacon and drippings over mixture and toss lightly. Serve at room temperature with melba toast or saltine crackers.

Yields 6 servings.

Fiesta Chicken Salad

1 3½- to 4-pound chicken, cooked and cut into bite-size pieces
½ cup chopped green olives with pimentos
1 cup celery, chopped
¼ cup dill pickles, chopped
¼ cup sweet pickles
6 eggs, hard-boiled and sliced
¼ cup half-and-half
½ cup mayonnaise
salt and pepper to taste
½ teaspoon garlic powder

Mix cream and mayonnaise. Combine all ingredients; toss lightly. Serve on lettuce and sliced tomatoes or as sandwiches or fill ½ chilled cantaloupe.

Yields 8 to 10 servings.

Fresh Green Bean and Chicken Salad

1½ pounds green beans, tops cut off
3 tablespoons red wine vinegar
⅓ cup olive oil, pure or extra virgin
1 tablespoon Dijon mustard
1 cup sweet red onions, thinly sliced
½ cup black olives, drained and sliced
1 cup cooked chicken or 8-ounce cooked chicken breast, cut in small cubes

Cook beans in salted water 15 minutes or until just crisp, drain and cool. In a mixing bowl, add vinegar, oil and mustard. Blend with a fork or wire whisk 2 or 3 minutes. Add onions, chicken and beans and gently toss until well coated. Season to taste. Serve on lettuce leaves at room temperature.

Yields 6 servings.

Chicken Salad Italienne

1 3½- to 4-pound chicken or turkey, cooked and cut into bite-size pieces
3 medium potatoes, boiled, peeled (optional) and diced
3 large eggs, hard-boiled and diced
1 medium sweet red onion, diced
3 tablespoons green olives, diced
1 2-ounce jar of pimentos
1 tablespoon leaf oregano
salt and pepper to taste
6 large lettuce leaves

*Combine all ingredients except lettuce in a large bowl. Salt and pepper to taste. Combine with **Italian Salad Dressing** and gently toss until all parts are coated. Arrange lettuce leaves on salad plates. Serve at room temperature with melba toast or crackers.*

Yields 6 servings.

Chicken Nut Salad

1 1/2 cups cooked chicken
2 tablespoons pine nuts, chopped
2 tablespoons pecans, chopped
3 tender stalks celery, cut in 3-inch julienne pieces
1/2 medium sweet red onion, sliced thin
3/4 cup black olives, sliced

Dressing:

1 1/4 tablespoon lemon juice
1/4 cup extra virgin olive oil
1/2 teaspoon black pepper
3/4 teaspoon salt
1/2 to 1 teaspoon garlic powder or to taste
1/4 to 1/2 teaspoon flaked red pepper or to taste

Place all ingredients except dressing in a mixing bowl and toss. Add salad dressing and toss again. Chill 2 hours. Arrange lettuce leaves on salad plates. Garnish with chopped parsley.

Yields 6 servings.

Chicken Spring Salad

1 3 1/2- to 4-pound chicken, cooked and cut into chunks
6 green onions, cut in thin slices about 1-inch long
1/2 cup mushrooms, sautéed
1 4-ounce can pimentos, cut into pieces
salt and pepper to taste
1/2 cup Italian dressing

Mix cold chicken, cold green beans, onions, mushrooms and pimentos; chill 1 hour. Thirty minutes before serving, add salad dressing and chill until serving time.

Yields 8 to 10 servings.

Chicken Twist Salad

1 3½- to 4-pound chicken, cooked and cut into bite-size pieces
8-ounce package Rotini twists, cooked
½ cup Italian dressing
½ cup mayonnaise
3 tablespoons lemon juice
1 tablespoon prepared mustard
1 medium onion, chopped
¾ cup ripe olive wedges
1 cup cucumbers, diced
1 cup celery, diced
1 teaspoon pepper

Mix pasta with chicken and Italian dressing. Cool. Blend mayonnaise, lemon juice and mustard. Stir in chopped onions, olives, cucumbers, celery and pepper. Add to pasta mixture. Salt to taste. Mix well. Chill 2 or more hours to blend flavor. Serve in lettuce cups.

Yields 6 to 8 servings.

Codfish Salad

1 pound codfish steak, 1-inch thick
salt and pepper
1½ cups celery hearts (inner stalks), cut in 1-inch pieces, including leaves
½ cup black ripe olives, sliced
2 tablespoons fresh parsley, chopped coarse
2 cloves garlic, minced
½ teaspoon flaked red pepper
1 teaspoon oregano

Blend together:

1 tablespoon fresh lemon
2 tablespoons wine vinegar
¼ cup extra virgin olive oil

Poach codfish in 1 cup of dry white wine, 1 bay leaf and salt to taste. Cook 7 to 8 minutes—fish should flake off easily, but firm with a fork. Drain, cool and separate into flakes. In a mixing bowl, add codfish and remaining ingredients. Toss gently. Chill and serve on lettuce leaves.

Yields 4 to 6 servings.

Sicilian Finger Salad

1 or 2 heads romaine lettuce, broken into separate leaves
1/4 cup wine vinegar
1/4 cup extra virgin olive oil
salt and pepper to taste
1 large clove garlic, finely minced

Place lettuce leaves in a large cotton towel and roll up loosely; chill 2 to 3 hours. Blend rest of ingredients. Place vinaigrette in a flat bowl and put in middle of a large serving platter. Arrange lettuce around the platter, the rib of lettuce facing out.

Yields 4 to 6 servings.

Sicilian Olive Salad

1 1/2 cups salad green olives, sliced
3/4 cup pitted black olives, sliced
1 medium sweet green bell pepper, cored and seeded
1 medium sweet red pepper, cored and seeded
3/4 cup plus 2 tablespoons extra virgin olive oil
1/4 cup fresh parsley, chopped coarse
1/4 cup dry white wine
1/4 cup wine vinegar

Cut peppers in 1/4-inch strips. Sauté in 2 tablespoons olive oil until limp; set aside. In a mixing bowl, combine rest of ingredients and mix. Add peppers and mix again until salad is well blended. Keep at room temperature. Serve as an appetizer or condiment with chicken or fish. Can also be used as a topping for Italian sub or hero sandwiches.

Pasta Salad

1 pound pasta twist, or shells
1 4-ounce jar pimentos
$^1/_2$ to $^2/_3$ cup **Marinade**
2 tablespoons chopped parsley and basil

Cook pasta al dente; drain immediately and wash with cold water until pasta is lukewarm. Place in a large mixing bowl and add marinade, pimentos, parsley and basil and gently mix. Adjust seasoning. Chill.

Yields 8 to 10 servings.

Italian Potato Salad

2 pounds new potatoes, cooked al dente with skins
2 tablespoons fresh parsley, chopped fine
1 teaspoon black pepper or to taste
1 teaspoon salt or to taste
$^{1}/_{2}$ teaspoon flaked red pepper (optional)
4 tablespoons extra virgin olive oil
3 tablespoons red wine vinegar

Cut potatoes into bite-size pieces in a mixing bowl; toss with rest of ingredients. Cover and chill several hours. Serve with broiled chicken.

Soybean Curd (Tofu), Peas and Bean Salad

1-pound package firm tofu packed in water, drained and cut in $^{1}/_{2}$ × 2-inch pieces
$^{1}/_{2}$ cup vegetable oil
1 10-ounce package frozen peas, thawed
1 10-ounce package cut green beans, thawed
2 tablespoons soy sauce
salt and pepper to taste
$^{1}/_{4}$ cup Italian salad dressing (your favorite)
$^{3}/_{4}$ teaspoon flaked red pepper (optional)

Heat oil in heavy frying pan and lightly brown tofu. Remove and drain on paper towels. Reserve 3 tablespoons oil; discard remainder. Sauté onions about 3 minutes; add peas, beans and soy sauce. Continue cooking 5 minutes. Add tofu. Stir 1 minute and adjust seasonings. Transfer tofu and vegetable mixture to serving bowl. Add salad dressing, blend and chill. Serve on lettuce leaves.

Yields 6 to 8 servings.

Soups

Arkansas Italian Chicken Veggie Soup

1 10-ounce package of the following frozen vegetables: peas and carrots, sliced okra, lima beans
1 large onion, chopped
1- to 1½-pounds fresh cabbage, cut up coarse
1 cup celery, chopped (include leaves)
1 28-ounce can tomatoes, chopped
1 cup dried Northern beans, soaked overnight or 1 16-ounce can Great Northern beans
3 large cloves garlic, chopped coarse
1 tablespoon oregano
1 tablespoon salt
1 teaspoon pepper
½ teaspoon flaked red pepper
2 tablespoons olive oil
3 or 4 chicken backs
2 quarts water

In a large soup pot, brown onions in olive oil. Add tomatoes and remainder of ingredients. Simmer. Remove light brown foam that rises to top. Adjust salt and pepper to taste. Simmer 1½ hours. Remove chicken backs and return meat to soup (no skin). Serve with cornbread or saltine crackers.

Yields 8 to 10 servings.

Bloody Mary Chicken Soup
Southern Style

2 chicken wings, 1 gizzard, 1 neck, 1 back
1 large onion, chopped
1 teaspoon flaked red pepper
2 cloves garlic, minced
2 tablespoons parsley, minced
3 tablespoons olive oil
$^1/_2$ cup dry white wine
1 eyedropper vodka (optional)
$^1/_2$ teaspoon black pepper
1 teaspoon salt
1 46-ounce can tomato juice
2 tablespoons rice
2 teaspoons oregano

In a 4- to 6-quart saucepan, lightly brown onion, garlic and parsley in olive oil. Add tomato juice, chicken parts and remaining ingredients, except rice. Bring to a boil and cover. Simmer 1 hour. Add rice and cook 20 minutes.

Yields 8 servings.

Chicken Soup

4 chicken backs
2 or 3 gizzards (optional)
1 cup celery, diced, include leaves
1 16-ounce can whole tomatoes, crushed
1 cup carrots, diced
1 cup yellow onion, diced
¹/₄ cup fresh parsley, chopped coarse
2 teaspoons salt or to taste
1 teaspoon black pepper or to taste

In a large soup pot, add 4 quarts water and all the ingredients listed. Bring to a slow boil, then simmer 1 hour, covered. Skim the light brown material off the top twice. Remove chicken backs and cool. Remove chicken meat and add to broth. Discard skin and bones, cut up gizzards and add to broth. For 6 servings, place 5 cups chicken broth in a medium pan and bring to a slow boil. Add ¹/₂ cup rice. Serve with grated Romano cheese and garnish with chopped fresh parsley. Remaining soup stock can be frozen for future use.

Variation:

Add ¹/₂ pound hamburger with salt, pepper and 1 tablespoon chopped parsley rolled into marble-size meatballs. Add 5 minutes before rice is done.

Wine selection: Frascati, a soft dry white

Leek and Potato Soup

1 bunch leeks, sliced thin, include some tails
4 medium potatoes, diced
1 large yellow onion, diced
3 cloves garlic, minced
salt and pepper to taste
3 cups chicken broth
1 cup dry white wine
2 cups half-and-half
¹/₄ cup parsley, minced

In a large soup pot, add water and all ingredients, except wine and cream. Bring to a boil, adjust seasonings and cover. Simmer 45 minutes and cool 15 minutes. Stir in wine and cream. Using a blender at medium speed, blend 3 cups soup mix 1 minute. Repeat until all the soup is blended. Reheat to very warm, garnish with parsley and serve.

Yields 10 to 12 servings.

Lentil Soup

1 pound lentils
³/₄ pound center cut ham slice, cubed in ¹/₂-inch pieces
1 large onion, sliced thin
1 cup carrots, ¹/₄-inch slices
salt and pepper to taste
3 tablespoons olive oil, extra virgin or pure
¹/₂ teaspoon flaked red pepper

In a heavy Dutch oven pot, brown onions in the olive oil. Add 3 quarts water and remaining ingredients. Simmer 1 hour. Adjust seasonings. Continue cooking until lentils are tender. Serve with green onion garnish and grated Romano or Parmesan cheese.

Yields 10 to 12 servings.

Wine selection: Rosatello Rose, a sweet, fruity red

Minestrone

3 large tomatoes, chopped coarse
3 carrots, sliced thin
3 zucchini, sliced thin
2 medium yellow onions, sliced thin
¹/₂ cup fresh parsley, chopped fine
1 cup fresh or frozen peas
1 cup celery, diced, include leaves
¹/₂ pound spinach, chopped coarse
¹/₂ pound escarole, chopped coarse
¹/₂ cup dry white beans
¹/₂ cup garbanzo beans (ceci)
¹/₂ cup fava (if available)
4 large cloves garlic, minced
2 bay leaves
1 tablespoon salt
1 teaspoon black pepper or to taste
6 quarts water or chicken stock
1 cup small elbow macaroni or favorite pasta
¹/₃ cup olive oil, extra virgin or pure

Soak beans overnight and then drain. Heat olive oil over medium to high heat in a 10-quart pot. Add onions and brown lightly. Add remaning ingredients, except pasta. Stir and bring to a boil. Reduce heat and simmer, covered 1¹/₂ hours or until beans are tender. Add pasta and cook 10 minutes. Serve with garnish of minced fresh basil and parsley and Parmesan or Romano cheese.

Yields 30 servings.

Wine selection: Fazi Battaglia, a smooth dry white

Roman Egg Soup

1 1/2 quarts chicken broth, fresh or canned
3 large eggs, beaten and seasoned with salt and pepper
1/2 cup Parmesan or Romano cheese, grated
1/2 pound mild Italian sausage, removed from casing and formed into marble-size meatballs
1/3 cup fresh parsley, chopped medium
1/3 cup angel hair pasta, broken into small pieces
salt and pepper to taste

Heat broth in a 4-quart pot. Bring to a boil and add pasta. Cook about 4 minutes (not quite done). Add sausage and cook 1 minute. Turn off heat. Add beaten eggs slowly and stir. Add parsley and cheese and stir until blended. Cool soup and serve in large soup bowls with crusty Italian bread.

Yields 10 servings.

Seafood Soup/Genovese

2 pounds boneless cod fillet, cut into large cubes
2 large onions, chopped coarse
2 leaks, chopped coarse, include some tails
2 large tomatoes, quartered
4 cloves garlic, quartered
several sprigs of fresh basil, if available
1/4 cup fresh parsley, chopped coarse
1/4 teaspoon fennel seed
2 bay leaves
1 cup dry white wine
2 1/2 quarts chicken broth or water
salt and pepper to taste
1/2 to 1 teaspoon red flaked pepper
1/4 cup Parmesan cheese, grated
4 ounces angel hair pasta, broken into small pieces
1/4 cup pure olive oil

In a large soup pot, sauté onions and leeks in olive oil until slightly browned. Add tomatoes and garlic, cook 2 to 3 minutes, add remaining ingredients, except cheese and pasta, bring to a slow boil and cook 25 minutes. Cover, remove from heat and let cool. Discard bay leaves. Put soup a few cups at a time in a blender or food processor and run at medium speed 2 minutes. Return to soup pot. Bring to a boil and add pasta (will be done in 5 to 6 minutes), remove from heat. Let cool a few minutes; add cheese, stir and serve. May be garnished with a mixture of fresh parsley and basil chopped fine.

Yields 16 to 18 servings.

Wine selection: Pinot Grigio, a crisp, flavorful dry white

Sicilian Fava Soup

1 pound fava beans, soaked overnight (navy, Great Northern or lima beans may be used)
1 pound pork spare ribs, cut in single ribs
1 pound Italian sausage, cut in 2-inch pieces
1/2 pound bacon, cut in 1-inch pieces
1/2 head green cabbage, shredded
1 bulb fennel, chopped or 4 stalks celery, cut in 1-inch pieces
3 large tomatoes, chopped
2 onions, sliced thin
salt and pepper to taste
3/4 teaspoon flaked red pepper
2 quarts chicken broth or water

In a large soup pot, brown sausage and ribs in 1/4 cup pure olive oil. Add bacon and vegetables and cook 5 minutes. Add soaked fava beans, water and seasonings. Bring to a boil, lower heat and simmer 1 1/2 hours covered. Adjust seasoning. If beans are not tender, cook an additional 20 minutes. Serve hot in large soup bowls with Italian bread.

Yields 6 to 8 servings.

Wine selection: Rubesco, a medium-bodied dry red

Sicilian Squash Soup

1 pound yellow squash, cut in 1-inch pieces
1 16-ounce can stewed tomatoes
1 large onion, quartered
1 cup chicken broth, fresh or canned
1/2 cup dry white wine
2 tablespoons extra virgin olive oil
1 teaspoon oregano
1 teaspoon salt
1/2 teaspoon pepper
2 large cloves garlic, quartered

Place all ingredients except wine in 4-quart pot and simmer 45 minutes, covered. Cool to room temperature. Place soup, 4 cups at a time, in a blender at medium speed 1 minute. Return to pot, add wine and heat to medium hot.

Yields 8 to 10 servings.

Zucchini Blender Soup

1½ pounds zucchini, cut in ½-inch chunks
1 pound tomatoes, chopped coarse
1 large yellow onion, sliced thin
3 tablespoons olive oil, extra virgin or pure
1½ teaspoons salt
½ teaspoon black pepper
1 tablespoon dried oregano
3 large cloves garlic, chopped coarse
1 cup dry white wine

In a 6-quart pot, brown onions in olive oil. Add all ingredients except wine. Add 4 cups water and simmer ½ hour covered. Let cool to warm; add wine and mix. Place contents in a blender at medium speed. Serve warm or at room temperature and garnish with chopped fresh parsley and grated Romano cheese.

Yields 10 servings.

Wine selection: Bardolino, a soft, light to medium-bodied dry red

Pasta and Sauces

There are many shapes and forms of pasta; each shape fits the sauce. Therefore, when you choose a specific pasta, have in mind the sauce needed. For example, a medium-thick white sauce calls for a wide pasta like fettuccine, while a medium-thin sauce works well with spaghetti or linguine. You need a thin sauce for tubular macaroni such as ziti, penne and rigatoni, so the sauce can flow into the openings.

At last count, there are 403 different pasta products in Italy, ranging in type from soup to lasagna. In the U.S., about 113 different pasta forms are available. Do you need a different sauce for each pasta? No; with experience you adapt 8 or 10 basic sauces to fit the pasta. Some of the more popular forms are: angel hair (very fine and cooks in 4 to 5 minutes), shells, bow ties, fusilli (spirals), manicotti (tubes for stuffing with ricotta mix), mostaciolli and rotini (twists).

Pick your pasta and sauce and a hearty Bon Appetito!

Perfect pasta is cooked al dente:

Bring 1 gallon water to a rolling boil; add 1 tablespoon salt and then slowly add 1 pound pasta. Stir until it becomes soft and returns to a rolling boil. This prevents the pasta from sticking together. Use a timer! Different brands have different cooking times. Subtract 2 minutes from cooking time recommended, then test a strand every 30 to 40 seconds until the pasta has a medium bite, but has resistance and is not soft. Don't forget that pasta continues to cook after you turn the heat off and drain the pasta. Toss immediately with the sauce and serve.

Fresh pasta cooks in less than half the time of packaged and needs to be watched closely since it will overcook very quickly.

Homemade Pasta

2 cups all-purpose flour
2 large eggs, slightly beaten
1/2 teaspoon salt
1 tablespoon olive oil, extra virgin or pure
1 tablespoon cold water

Pour flour into a large mixing bowl or on a smooth work surface. Make a well in the middle, add eggs, salt, oil and water. Mix together with a fork or your fingers until the dough can be gathered into a rough ball.

To make pasta by hand:

Knead dough on floured work surface about 10 minutes. Dough will be smooth, shiny and elastic. Divide dough into 4 balls and let rest 10 minutes. Using a heavy rolling pin, roll the dough into thin sheets and cut in 10- to 12-inch strips. Roll up each strip like a jelly roll and cut in 1/4-inch widths. Unravel pasta on a clean cloth to dry 1/2 to 1 hour.

To make pasta by machine:

The machine will do the kneading, rolling and cutting. Set the rollers as far apart as possible. Feed dough through rollers 4 or 5 times folding dough each time. Flour lightly if dough is sticky. When dough is smooth and shiny it is ready. Now set dough to the second notch and roll it out. Continue to close rollers until pasta is 1/16-inch thick. Set machine to cut fettuccine and place on a clean cloth to dry.

Quickie Twenty Minute Sauce

1 16-ounce can tomato sauce
1 16-ounce can whole tomatoes, crushed
1 medium onion, sliced thin
1 1/2 teaspoons dried oregano
1 1/2 teaspoons dried basil
1/2 teaspoon garlic powder
3 tablespoons olive oil, extra virgin or pure
2 tablespoons fresh parsley, chopped coarse
1 teaspoon salt
1/2 teaspoon black pepper

In a 10-inch skillet with medium-high heat, add oil. Sauté onions 5 minutes; add remaining ingredients and blend. Reduce heat and simmer 15 minutes uncovered. Meanwhile, have a large pot of water boiling and cook 1 pound of your favorite pasta al dente. Drain and toss with 1/2 of the sauce. Serve with grated Parmesan or Romano cheese.

Yields 4 to 6 servings.

Sicilian Marinara Sauce II

2 16-ounce cans tomato sauce
1 16-ounce can whole tomatoes, crushed
1 large onion, sliced thin
2 teaspoons dried oregano
1 teaspoon dried basil or 1 tablespoon fresh
1 teaspoon garlic powder
$1/4$ cup olive oil, extra virgin or pure
$1/4$ cup fresh parsley, chopped coarse
1 teaspoon salt or to taste
$3/4$ teaspoon black pepper
$1/2$ to 1 teaspoon flaked red pepper or to taste

In a large skillet over medium-high heat, sauté onions 5 minutes. Add remaining ingredients, stir, reduce heat and simmer 15 minutes. Cook 1 pound of your favorite pasta al dente, drain and toss with $1/2$ of the sauce. Serve with grated Parmesan or Romano cheese.

Variations:

Red Clam Sauce—After sauce has cooked 5 minutes, add 1 10-ounce or 2 6$1/2$-ounce cans of baby minced clams, including juice and simmer 10 minutes. Toss with 1 pound cooked pasta al dente.

Red Shrimp Sauce—After sauce has cooked 9 minutes, add 1 pound of peeled, deveined small or medium shrimp and simmer 6 minutes. Toss with 1 pound of your favorite pasta al dente.

Red Anchovy Sauce—Add 2 2-ounce cans anchovies, mashed to sauce during last 5 minutes of cooking time. Toss with 1 pound of large shells al dente.

Yields 5 to 6 servings.

Wine selection: Red Zinfandel, a fruity, medium-bodied dry red

Forty-five Minute Meat Sauce

2 15-ounce cans tomato sauce

1 15-ounce can whole tomatoes, crushed

1 medium yellow onion, sliced thin

1 1/2 teaspoons dried oregano

1 teaspoon dried basil

1 teaspoon dried garlic powder

3 tablespoons olive oil, extra virgin or pure

2 tablespoons fresh parsley, chopped coarse

1 teaspoon salt

1/2 teaspoon black pepper

1 bell pepper, seeded and cut into small pieces

2 cups mushrooms, sliced

1 pound lean hamburger meat, well browned, fat drained off in colander

Parmesan or Romano cheese, grated

In a 4-quart pot, sauté onions, bell pepper and mushrooms in olive oil 7 to 8 minutes. Add remaining ingredients and bring to a slow boil; cover and simmer 30 minutes. Uncover and cook 5 minutes. Cook 1 pound of pasta al dente, which will be tossed with 1/4 of the sauce. Sprinkle with cheese.

Yields 5 to 6 servings.

Wine selection: Gallo Burgundy, a flavorful dry red

Two Hour + Gourmet Tomato Sauce

1- to 1½-pounds beef neck bones
1- to 1½-pounds pork neck bones
4 16-ounce cans tomato sauce
1 28-ounce can whole tomatoes, crushed
1 6-ounce can tomato paste
4 large cloves garlic, minced
3 tablespoons fresh parsley, chopped coarse
2½ tablespoons dried oregano
1½ tablespoons dried basil
1 tablespoon salt or to taste
1 teaspoon black pepper or to taste
1 large or 2 medium onions, sliced thin
1 large bell pepper, seeded and cut into small pieces
2 cups mushrooms, sliced
¼ cup olive oil, extra virgin or pure
Meatballs

*In a 10-quart Dutch oven or pot, sauté in olive oil onions, bell peppers and mushrooms 8
minutes. Add tomatoes, sauce and paste. Blend and simmer 10 minutes. Add seasonings and
parsley.*

*Add remaining ingredients. Bring to a slow boil; simmer 1½ hours, stirring occasionally.
Uncover and simmer an additional 15 minutes. Remove neck bones and let cool; remove
any meat and put back into sauce. Take out meatballs and keep warm. Meanwhile, cook 2
pounds of your favorite pasta al dente. Top with 4 cups of the sauce. Put 3 cups of the sauce
in a bowl and pass around to be used as needed along with grated Parmesan or Romano
cheese. Serve the pasta with the meatballs and green salad for a great Sicilian meal.*

Yields 10 to 12 servings.

Wine selection: Chianti Classico Riserva, a medium-bodied dry red

Meatballs

2 pounds lean hamburger or chuck
2 large eggs, slightly beaten
4 slices day old white bread, soaked in water (squeeze out excess)
2 teaspoons salt or to taste
1 teaspoon pepper or to taste
1 teaspoon garlic powder

In a mixing bowl, combine all ingredients and blend with fingers thoroughly. Wet hands, pinch off piece of meat about the size of 2 golf balls and roll in palm until round. Preheat large, non-stick frying pan to medium-high heat and brown the meatballs. Drain on paper towels. Add to **Fresh Tomato Sauce I.**

Yields 22 meatballs.

Pesto Sauce

Pesto sauce originated in Northwest Italy and has become popular everywhere, including the U.S.A. To make good pesto you must use fresh basil, which is not readily available in most areas. Pesto can also be made with either all parsley, all fresh spinach leaves or a combination of ¹/₂ parsley and ¹/₂ spinach. Another variation is ¹/₃ parsley, ¹/₃ basil and ¹/₃ spinach. All are excellent and during those cold winter days, pesto sauce tossed with pasta brings springtime into your kitchen.

Variations:

To 1 cup of half-and-half add 2 tablespoons pesto sauce. Heat to simmer 5 minutes and cool for dip or serve hot over fish or steak.

For veggie dip—Blend 1 16-ounce carton sour cream, ¹/₂ cup milk and 2 tablespoons pesto sauce.

Pesto Sauce According to M & S

1 cup fresh parsley leaves, tightly packed (prefer flat-leaf Italian type), chopped coarse
2 cups fresh basil leaves (no stems), tightly packed and chopped coarse
1¼ teaspoons salt
¾ teaspoons black pepper
5 large cloves garlic, chopped coarse
3 tablespoons pine nuts or chopped walnuts
1½ cups olive oil, extra virgin or pure
¾ cup Romano or Parmesan cheese, grated

Add all ingredients in a blender except basil, parsley and cheese. Blend 1 minute, then slowly add basil and parsley handful at a time and blend at high speed; add cheese. Store in a covered quart Mason jar in refrigerator. Use 4 rounded tablespoons of pesto sauce for 1 pound pasta. Can be used on meats; mix with equal parts of light cream. Or serve for breakfast on dry toast.

Fresh Tomato Sauce I

3 tablespoons olive oil, extra virgin or pure
5 medium tomatoes or Roma (Italian pear-shaped) tomatoes, cut in ½-inch pieces
1 medium green pepper, chopped coarse
2 bunches green scallions, cut in 1-inch pieces including ½ of the green tails
1 teaspoon salt or to taste
1 teaspoon pepper or to taste
2 rounded tablespoons parsley, chopped
2 rounded tablespoons fresh oregano, chopped or 1½ teaspoons dry
2 rounded tablespoons fresh basil, chopped or 2 teaspoons dry
8 ounces fresh mushrooms, sliced and quartered
2 cloves garlic, minced

Sauté onions, mushrooms and pepper in olive oil over medium- high heat 5 to 6 minutes. Mix tomatoes with remaining ingredients, add to onions and pepper and bring to a boil. Reduce heat and cook 10 minutes; do not cover. Meanwhile, cook 1 pound of your favorite pasta al dente. Drain and place on a serving platter. Pour sauce over pasta and serve with grated Parmesan or Romano cheese.

Yields 5 to 6 servings.

Wine selection: Catullo Bianco, a tart, crisp dry white

Fresh Tomato Sauce II

3 pounds tomatoes, chopped
3 cloves garlic, minced
3 tablespoons fresh basil, chopped
3 tablespoons fresh parsley, chopped (Italian or single leaf preferred)
3 tablespoons olive oil, pure or extra virgin
1 1/2 teaspoons salt or to taste
1 teaspoon pepper or to taste

In a large heavy skillet, heat oil over medium heat and sauté garlic 10 seconds; add basil and parsley. Stir and cook 20 seconds; add tomatoes and salt and pepper. Stir and cook uncovered 15 minutes. Pour over 1 pound of cooked pasta al dente and serve with grated Parmesan cheese.

Yields 5 to 6 servings.

Wine selection: Orvietto Classico, a fruity, light to medium-bodied dry white

Sixty Seconds Fresh Tomato Sauce III

3 pounds tomatoes, chopped coarse
1/3 cup olive oil, extra virgin or pure
3 medium-large cloves garlic, minced
1/3 cup fresh parsley, chopped coarse
1/3 cup fresh basil (if available), chopped coarse
salt and pepper to taste
1 pound pasta, cooked al dente

In a large heavy skillet, heat oil and sauté garlic 30 seconds. Add tomatoes and parsley, season with salt and pepper, stir to blend and turn off heat. The pasta should be cooked, drained and returned to the pot at the time you heat the oil for making the sauce. Pour the tomato sauce over the pasta and toss. Serve with grated Parmesan or Romano cheese and garnish with basil.

Yields 6 servings.

Wine selection: Torre di Giano, a fruity, medium-bodied dry white with a touch of oakiness

Italian White Sauce

6 tablespoons olive oil, extra virgin or pure or 6 tablespoons melted butter
3¹/₂ tablespoons flour
4 cups half-and-half, warmed
1 teaspoon salt (optional)
1 teaspoon black pepper or to taste
1 teaspoon pure garlic powder
1 cup Parmesan cheese, grated

Mix cheese, flour and spices; set aside. Over medium heat in heavy skillet, heat olive oil 2 to 3 minutes. Stir in flour and cheese mixture, stirring constantly until it dissolves. Do not brown. When it is bubbly, add warm cream, slowly stirring constantly and bring to a boil; cook 5 minutes. Immediately pour over 1¹/₂ pounds cooked linguine or fettuccine al dente. Toss and serve.

Variations:

Sauté 12 ounces of sliced mushrooms in olive oil and add to sauce when you add the cream.

Sauté 1 pound of small to medium shrimp in olive oil about 6 minutes and add to sauce when you add the cream.

Add 3 6¹/₂-ounce cans of minced or baby clams to sauce when you add the cream—this makes the famous clam sauce.

Yields 8 to 10 servings.

Wine selection: Bolla Chardonnay, a pleasant dry white

Sicilian Pasta Primavera

3 pounds tomatoes, coarsely chopped (Italian pear-shaped tomatoes preferred)
1 large yellow onion, thinly sliced
1 bunch green onions, cut in 1-inch pieces, including tails
3 cloves garlic, minced
$^1/_4$ cup fresh parsley, chopped coarse
1 cup fresh mushrooms, sliced
1 cup broccoli florets
1 cup cauliflower florets
1 cup zucchini, sliced
2 teaspoons salt or to taste
$^1/_2$ teaspoon black pepper or to taste
$^1/_2$ teaspoon red pepper flakes (optional)
2 teaspoons dried oregano
1 teaspoon dried basil or 3 tablespoons fresh, chopped
$^1/_4$ cup extra virgin or pure olive oil
1 pound cooked linguine or fettuccine al dente

In a large frying pan over medium-high heat, sauté onions in olive oil 3 minutes. Add garlic, parsley and green onions; sauté an additional 3 minutes. Add chopped tomatoes and all seasonings. Add $^1/_2$ cup water. Bring to a boil, lower heat and cook 5 minutes. Add vegetables and mushrooms, stir and cook covered an additional 8 minutes. Toss pasta with $^1/_3$ of sauce. Arrange on a warm platter and spread remaining sauce evenly over pasta. Serve piping hot with grated Parmesan or Romano cheese.

(For variety other vegetables may be substituted: green beans, green peas, snow peas, yellow squash, etc.)

Yields 6 servings.

Wine selection: Corvo Rosso, a medium-bodied dry red

Pasta/Eggs & Herbs

1 pound linguine, cooked al dente
2 large eggs, hard-boiled, peeled and chopped
¼ cup olive oil, pure or extra virgin
2 cloves garlic, minced
⅓ cup fresh parsley, chopped coarse
salt and pepper to taste

In a heavy skillet over medium-high heat, add oil and garlic. Stir and cook 20 seconds. Add chopped eggs, stir and cook 1 minute. Add parsley and cook 30 seconds. Pour over pasta and toss. Serve with fresh garden salad and Italian bread.

Yields 6 servings.

Wine selection: Corvo Bianco, a dry white

Pasta and Zucchini

1 pound pasta, cooked al dente
4 medium zucchini, sliced in ¼-inch rounds and sprinkled with seasoned salt
½ cup Parmesan cheese, grated
½ cup pure divided olive oil
4 cups *Forty-five Minute Meat Sauce*

In a large skillet, sauté zucchini in oil on each side until golden brown. Drain on paper towels. Arrange on cookie sheets and sprinkle with cheese. Toss pasta with 2 cups sauce. In a serving bowl, add ⅓ pasta. Cover with ⅓ zucchini. Spoon some sauce over zucchini. Repeat until all ingredients are used, ending with zucchini on top.

Yields 6 servings.

Wine selection: Taurasi, a full-bodied dry red

Pasta with Porcini Mushrooms

1 ounce dried or fresh porcini mushrooms
$^1/_2$ cup pure olive oil
3 cloves garlic, chopped medium
$^1/_2$ pound small shrimp, shelled and cleaned
1 pound pasta, cooked al dente

Cut mushrooms into small pieces and cook in $^1/_4$ cup water 5 minutes; set aside. In a heavy skillet over medium heat, sauté garlic in 2 tablespoons oil about 30 seconds. Add remaining oil, mushrooms and liquid. Simmer 5 minutes. Add shrimp and simmer 6 minutes. Season with salt and pepper or seasoned salt. Cook 1 minute. Toss with cooked pasta and serve immediately with garlic bread and fresh green salad.

Yields 6 servings.

Wine selection: Chardonnay Lungarotti, a medium-bodied dry white

Pasta-Alio-Olio

1 pound of your favorite pasta, cooked al dente
$^1/_4$ cup olive oil, extra virgin or pure
2 to 4 cloves garlic, crushed in a small frying pan

Add oil to frying pan with garlic and slowly heat to medium-high heat. Simmer 1 to 2 minutes; stir. Pour oil and garlic mix over pasta and toss; discard cloves of garlic. Serve on a warm platter with Romano or Parmesan cheese and a Sicilian tomato salad.

Yields 6 servings.

Wine selection: Chianti, a dry red

Mom's Pasta e Fagioli

¹/₂ pound dried white beans, soaked overnight
2 quarts chicken broth or liquid from soaked beans and enough water to make 2 quarts
1 large yellow onion, sliced thin
¹/₄ cup olive oil, extra virgin or pure
1 cup celery, cut in ¹/₂-inch pieces, include leaves
2 large tomatoes, chopped coarse
1 tablespoon oregano
¹/₂ teaspoon flaked red pepper
salt and pepper to taste .
¹/₄ cup parsley, chopped coarse
3 large cloves garlic, minced
1 pound of your favorite pasta, uncooked

In a large pot, brown onions in olive oil. Add chicken broth or water and remaining ingredients except pasta. Cook until beans are tender, about 1¹/₂ to 2 hours. Add pasta and cook al dente. Serve in soup bowls. Sprinkle with grated Romano cheese.

Yields 6 servings.

Wine selection: Valpolicella, a soft, light-bodied dry red

Stuffed Jumbo Shells

12-ounce package jumbo shells

Filling:

1 cup mozarella cheese, shredded
1 cup Parmesan cheese, grated
2 pounds ricotta cheese
4 large eggs, beaten
1 teaspoon pepper
1 teaspoon garlic powder

Blend all ingredients. Use about 2 tablespoons per shell. Cook shells in 6 quarts salted water 8 minutes. Drain hot water and immediately cool with cold water. Drain and place shells on paper towels, open face down. Place a thin layer of your favorite tomato sauce on bottom of 12 × 9 × 2-inch baking pan. Stuff shells and place them open end up in pan in single layer. Cover with tomato sauce. Loosely cover with aluminum foil and bake in a preheated 375° oven 40 minutes.

Yields 12 to 13 servings.

Wine selection: Bevsano Barolo, a medium to full-bodied red

Poultry

Chicken Liver Sauce Caruso

1 pound chicken livers, cut in 2 pieces

1/2 pound mushrooms, sliced

1 medium onion, chopped

2 15-ounce cans tomato sauce

2 teaspoons oregano

1 teaspoon basil

1 teaspoon garlic powder (more if desired)

2 tablespoons parsley, chopped

1 1/2 teaspoons salt

1 teaspoon black pepper

Sauté onion in 3 tablespoons olive oil. Pour in tomato sauce. Blend tomatoes, spices and parsley and simmer 10 minutes. In another pan, sauté mushrooms and chicken livers in 1/4 cup olive oil. Salt and pepper to taste. Combine the 2 mixtures and let simmer 10 minutes. This makes enough sauce for 1 pound of cooked spaghetti or linguine al dente.

Yields 6 servings.

Wine selection: Sebaste Barolo, a robust dry red

Weight Watchers' Chicken Livers

1 pound chicken livers

1 large onion, cut in rings

1 green pepper, cut in rings

3 cups tomato juice

1 teaspoon garlic powder

1 teaspoon pepper

3/4 teaspoon salt

Lightly salt and pepper chicken livers and place in a 6 × 9-inch baking dish. Brown green peppers and onions in small amount of oil. Mix in 3 cups tomato juice, salt and pepper and garlic powder. Pour over chicken livers. Bake in 350° oven 20 to 25 minutes. Serve over a bed of rice.

Yields 6 servings.

Chicken Glasnost

Commemorates Reagan-Gorbachev historic summit in Moscow, June 1988.

1 3- to 3¹/₂-pound chicken, cut into 9 or 10 serving pieces
1¹/₂ pounds pork tenderloin, cut in ¹/₄-inch rounds
1¹/₂ cups flour, seasoned
3 cups red cabbage, shredded
3 cups white cabbage, shredded
2 cups Irish potatoes, cubed and unpeeled
2 cups yellow onions, chopped coarse
3 cups tomatoes, chopped coarse
1 large cucumber, peeled, quartered and cut in ¹/₂-inch pieces
¹/₂ cup wine vinegar
¹/₂ cup vegetable oil, divided
5 cloves garlic, minced
1 tablespoon salt or to taste
1 teaspoon black pepper or to taste
1 teaspoon flaked red pepper
3 bay leaves
8 cups chicken or beef stock
fresh dill, chopped fine

In a large stew pot, brown onions in vegetable oil. Coat tenderloin and chicken in flour, shake off excess and lightly brown in vegetable oil. Combine browned meat and remainder of ingredients, except for dill, with onions in the stew pot. Bring to a boil, adjust seasonings and simmer 1 hour. Remove chicken, cool and debone. Return chicken to pot, blend and serve in deep soup dishes; garnish with fresh dill. Serve with Russian black bread and San Francisco sour dough bread.

Yields 10 servings.

Wine selection: Nebbiolo D' Alba, a peppery, medium-bodied dry red

Nixon Peking Chicken

Commemorates President Nixon's trip to China in 1973.

2 pounds boned chicken breast
2 tablespoons flour
2 teaspoons sugar
Accent (MSG)
6 to 7 tablespoons soy sauce
3 tablespoons dry vermouth
4 medium green bell peppers
1 teaspoon garlic powder
8 tablespoons vegetable oil
salt and pepper

Cut boned chicken strips about 2 inches long and ¹/₄ inch wide, salt and pepper to taste and sprinkle with Accent. Combine flour and sugar, blend with soy sauce and vermouth, mix with chicken and set aside to marinate. Cut green peppers in 1¹/₂-inch pieces. Pour about 4 tablespoons of oil into skillet on high heat. Add about ¹/₂ teaspoon salt, then green peppers. Stir constantly until peppers turn darker green, about 2 minutes. Remove green peppers leaving as much oil in skillet as possible. Add remaining oil to skillet with garlic powder. Stir in chicken mixture. Cook turning constantly 5 minutes. Add green peppers, mix well. Serve immediately with rice.

Yields 4 to 6 servings.

Wine selection: Sauvignon Blanc, a dry white

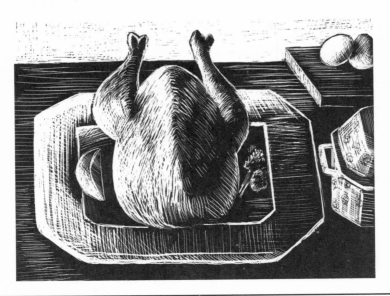

Chicken and Wine Sauce

1 3- to 3¹/₂-pound chicken, cut in serving pieces
1 cup white wine
¹/₄ cup pure olive oil
1 teaspoon garlic powder
2 tablespoons parsley, minced
2 tablespoons oregano
salt and pepper
1 pound Rotini pasta
¹/₂ cup Parmesan cheese

Pour olive oil on bottom of baking dish. Salt and pepper chicken and place in 1 layer. Pour white wine over chicken and sprinkle with parsley, oregano and garlic powder. Bake in preheated oven at 350° 1 to 1¹/₄ hours, depending on size of chicken. Turn over after first 30 minutes. Cook Rotini pasta al dente. Drain. Place chicken on serving dish. Srinkle Parmesan cheese and pour drippings and scrapings from baking pan on pasta and mix thoroughly. Serve immediately with chicken.

Yields 6 to 8 servings.

Wine selection: Soave, a crisp dry white

Chicken Stuffed Tufoli

Chicken Meat Filling:

2 pounds boned chicken breast, ground
1 large egg
2 slices of bread, soaked in milk
2 teaspoons salt
1 teaspoon pepper
1 teaspoon garlic powder
Quickie Twenty Minute Sauce
2 8-ounce packages tufoli, cooked al dente

Blend all ingredients together and set aside. Pour 1 cup tomato sauce over bottom of 9 × 12-inch baking dish. Stuff chicken meat firmly in each individual tufoli and place side by side in baking dish. Cover generously with more tomato sauce and sprinkle with Parmesan cheese. Cover pan with aluminum foil, bake in 350° oven 40 minutes. Remove from oven and let stand 10 minutes before serving. Use ¹/₄ cup hot tomato sauce on each serving.

Yields 8 to 10 servings.

Wine selection: Rosso di Montalcino, a fruity, medium-bodied dry red

Deviled Chicken

4 legs
3 thighs
3 breasts
salt and pepper
2 tablespoons pure olive oil
½ cup dry red wine
1 teaspoon instant mixed onion
1 teaspoon prepared mustard
1 bay leaf
1 teaspoon lemon juice
1 tablespoon cornstarch
½ cup sour cream

Salt and pepper chicken to taste and brown in hot oil. Add wine, onion, mustard, bay leaves and lemon juice. Cover and bake at 325° about 1 hour. Thicken juice with cornstarch. Stir in sour cream. Heat thoroughly; do not boil. Serve over rice.

Yields 6 servings.

Wine selection: Castello della Sala, a fruity, crisp dry white

Chicken Capri

6 drumsticks
6 thighs
3 breasts, halved
2 cups dry white wine
1½ cups sour cream
1 8-ounce can mushrooms (stems and pieces), drained
1 stick butter or oleo

Melt butter in electric skillet set at 350°. Salt and pepper each piece of chicken and brown evenly on each side. Arrange chicken in 1 layer in skillet and reduce heat to 250°. Pour 1 cup of wine over chicken and cover. Cook 40 minutes. Turn chicken occasionally. Mix remaining 1 cup of wine, sour cream and mushrooms and pour mixture over chicken evenly. Cover and cook 15 minutes. Remove chicken to serving platter. Cook 2 cups of rice, add gravy from skillet and mix thoroughly. Serve rice and chicken with green vegetable and salad.

Yields 6 to 8 servings.

Wine selection: Charles Shaw Gamay, a light, fruity dry red

Quick Creamed Chicken on Cornbread

3 cups cooked chicken or turkey, chopped in 1-inch pieces
3 cups whole milk
1/4 cup margarine or butter
1/4 cup all-purpose flour
1 pan of hot cornbread, cut in 3-inch squares
salt and pepper to taste

In a large skillet, melt margarine over medium-high heat. Add flour and stir with a wire wisk until blended and bubbly. Do not brown. Add milk, stir and cook 1 minute. Adjust seasoning with salt and pepper. Add chicken, stir and cook over low heat 7 to 8 minutes. Serve over hot cornbread or buttermilk biscuits.

Yields 6 to 8 servings.

Easy Chicken—Al Furno

1 3 1/2-pound chicken, cut into pieces
1/2 cup flour
2 teaspoons salt
1/2 teaspoon pepper
1 stick margarine
1 10 1/2-ounce can condensed cream of chicken soup
1/2 cup milk
1/2 cup sliced green olives
1 cup mushrooms, sliced
1 pimento, chopped
1 can biscuits

Roll chicken in mixture of flour, salt and pepper. Melt butter in 9 × 12-inch pan. Add chicken skin side down. Bake at 375° 45 minutes, turning chicken once. Combine soup, milk, olives, mushrooms and pimentos. Pour over chicken; place biscuits on top. Bake 10 to 12 minutes or until biscuits are golden brown. Serve hot.

Yields 6 to 8 servings.

Chicken Leg Casserole

6 chicken legs
6 chicken thighs
1/4 cup butter
1 can mushroom soup
1 4-ounce can mushrooms
1 2-ounce can pimentos
1/2 cup whipping cream
1/2 teaspoon garlic powder
salt and pepper to taste

Salt and pepper each piece and brown the chicken in the butter. Place in a casserole dish. Mix together the mushroom soup, mushrooms, pimentos, garlic, salt and whipping cream. Pour over chicken and bake 1 hour at 350°. Place the chicken pieces on a bed of rice and pour the remaining juice over the chicken and rice.

Yields 6 servings.

Holiday Chicken Roll

1 1/2 cups self-rising flour
1/2 cup shortening
1 large egg, beaten
3 tablespoons milk
1 cup cooked chicken, diced
1 4-ounce can mushrooms
1 2-ounce can pimentos, chopped
2 teaspoons parsley, minced
3 tablespoons soy sauce
1 can cream of chicken soup
salt and pepper

Place flour in mixing bowl and cut in shortening. Combine egg and milk; add to flour mixture, stirring until dough forms a ball. Chill dough. Combine chicken, mushrooms, pimentos, parsley, soy sauce and half the soup. Salt and pepper to taste and mix well. Divide dough into 2 parts. Roll each part to a rectangle. Spread with chicken mixture and roll dough as for jelly roll. Seal ends. Place in greased baking dish. Bake at 375° 25 to 30 minutes. Combine remaining soup and 1/2 cup water in saucepan. Stir over low heat until blended. Serve over chicken roll.

Yields 8 servings.

Chicken Oriental

3 whole chicken breasts, boned and cut in half
3 large green peppers, cut into strips or squares
6 slices canned pineapple, cut into squares
garlic powder
1 can cream of chicken soup, mixed with ½ can warm water
2 tablespoons soy sauce
⅓ cup cider vinegar
½ cup sugar
1 stick of butter

Salt and pepper chicken breasts and sprinkle lightly with garlic powder. Brown chicken in butter and place in a baking dish. Brown green peppers and pineapple until peppers are softened. Add soy sauce, vinegar, sugar and chicken soup to pineapple and green peppers, stir and simmer 10 minutes. Pour over chicken breasts and bake 45 minutes in a 350° preheated oven. Turn once after 30 minutes. Serve on a bed of rice.

Yields 6 servings.

Chicken Hong Kong

1 3½- to 4-pound chicken, cooked
3 cups chicken stock
3 tablespoons flour
1 16-ounce can bean sprouts or fresh
1 large can chow mein noodles
1 4-ounce can mushrooms (stems and pieces)
salt and pepper to taste

Remove meat from bones after cooking and cut into small chunks. Drain bean sprouts and mushrooms and mix with chicken chunks. Thicken chicken stock with flour and mix with chicken chunks, bean sprouts and mushrooms. Put ½ can of noodles in a buttered casserole dish, put chicken mixture over the noodles and sprinkle the remaining half of noodles on top. Bake in 400° oven about 20 minutes.

Yields 10 servings.

Spanish Chicken

1 3- to 3½-pound chicken, cut into pieces
¼ cup pure olive oil
1 #2 can tomatoes (2½ cups), drained
½ cup onion, chopped
½ cup green peppers, chopped
1 teaspoon oregano
1 teaspoon garlic powder
1 tablespoon salt
½ teaspoon pepper
¾ cup regular white rice
1 cup ripe olives, cut in large pieces
2 cups juice drained from tomatoes plus water

In a large skillet, brown chicken in olive oil. Add tomatoes, chopped onions, green pepper, oregano, garlic powder, salt and pepper. Simmer 5 minutes. Pour into 3-quart casserole dish. In same skillet cook rice in 2 tablespoons oil, stirring until golden brown and add with tomato juice to chicken. Bake at 350° about ½ hour or until chicken is tender and rice is cooked. Toss in olives and bake 5 minutes.

Yields 6 servings.

Imperial Chicken

1 stick margarine
4 chicken breasts
4 chicken thighs
4 chicken legs

Crumb mixture:

2 cups bread crumbs
¾ cup Romano cheese or Parmesan, grated
¼ cup parsley, chopped
1 clove garlic, minced
1 teaspoon salt
¼ teaspoon pepper

Dip chicken into melted margarine and then into crumb mixture. Bake in greased casserole dish 1 hour in open pan at 350°.

Yields 6 servings.

Chicken and Rice Supreme

3 chicken breasts, cut in half
6 chicken thighs or drumsticks
1 15-ounce can tomato sauce with bits
$^1/_2$ can water
1 tablespoon flour
1 teaspoon pepper
1 large onion, chopped coarse
1 green pepper, chopped coarse
$^1/_2$ teaspoon salt

Sprinkle chicken with salt and pepper to taste, then roll in dry bread crumbs. Brown in heavy skillet or dutch oven in $^1/_3$ cup oil. Mix salt, pepper, water and tomato sauce and pour over browned chicken. Add onion and green pepper, cover and cook over low heat 1 hour. Remove chicken and thicken tomato sauce with flour. Serve over rice.

Yields 6 servings.

Chicken—S.A.

4 cups cooked chicken or turkey, shredded
2 cans chicken soup
1 can chicken broth
1 cup tomato sauce
1 cup cheddar cheese, grated
$^1/_2$ cup green mild chili peppers, chopped
1 4-ounce can mushroom stems and pieces
1 package of 12 tortillas

Cut up 3 tortillas in $^1/_2$-inch strips. In a buttered casserole dish, place a layer of tortillas and a layer of chicken. Mix soup, broth, peppers, tomato sauce, mushrooms and onions. Pour some mixture over chicken. Add a layer of grated cheese. Alternate making 3 layers, ending with grated cheese. Cook 45 minutes in 375° oven. Serve with Mexican salad and hot rolls.

Yields 6 servings.

Sweetheart Chicken

1 large eggplant, peeled and sliced ⅓-inch thick
2 pounds raw chicken breasts, ground
1 15-ounce can tomato sauce
2 medium onions, chopped fine
2 teaspoons oregano
1 teaspoon garlic powder
4 tablespoons Parmesan cheese
½ cup flour
2 tablespoons parsley, finely chopped
salt and pepper to taste

Salt, pepper and flour lightly eggplant slices and brown quickly in olive oil over high heat. Place on paper towels to drain. Sauté onion lightly in small amount of oil. Add 2 pounds ground chicken. Salt and pepper to taste; brown lightly. Pour off excess grease. Add tomato sauce, oregano and garlic powder. Let simmer until liquids have mostly evaporated.

Put layer of eggplant in 9 × 12-inch baking pan, sprinkle with 2 tablespoons Parmesan cheese, add ½ of chicken mixture and pour over half of **Cream Sauce.** *Add another layer of eggplant and remaining half of chicken mixture; pour remaining cream sauce evenly over chicken, sprinkle with 2 tablespoons of Parmesan cheese. Bake 30 minutes at 325° then turn oven to 400° and bake another 10 minutes or until casserole is brown. Remove from oven and let stand 10 minutes. Arrange chopped parsley in shape of a heart.*

Yields 8 to 10 servings.

Wine selection: Boscani Pinot Grigio, a fruity, crisp dry white

Cream Sauce

3 cups milk
4 eggs
⅜ cup flour
1½ tablespoons butter

Heat 2½ cups milk and butter in a 2-quart saucepan; beat remaining milk, eggs and flour. Cook over low heat while slowly pouring in hot milk and butter. Stir constantly until mixture comes to a boil. Cook slowly until well thickened.

Valentine Salad

Mix together 1 package strawberry Jello and 1 cup hot water. Add 1 16-ounce can whole cranberry sauce. Let it cool. Add ½ pint sour cream and ½ cup nuts; pour in heart-shaped Jello pan and chill. Serve with **Sweetheart Chicken.**

Italian Diet Chicken

3-pound chicken, cut in pieces
1 bottle of diet Italian salad dressing
1 cup bread crumbs
salt and pepper

Salt and pepper chicken pieces to taste. Dip in salad dressing and then into bread crumbs. Place pieces in 9 × 12-inch baking dish. Pour remaining salad dressing over chicken. Bake in 350° oven 1 hour. Serve over a bed of rice.

Yields 4 to 6 servings.

Broiled Chicken Breasts

$2/3$ cup dry bread crumbs
$1/3$ cup Parmesan cheese
1 teaspoon garlic powder
pepper to taste
2 tablespoons fresh parsley, chopped
8 boneless, skinless chicken fillets, pounded flat
$1/4$ cup olive oil
salt and pepper to taste

Combine bread crumbs, Parmesan cheese, garlic powder, pepper and chopped parsley. Lightly salt and pepper chicken breasts, dip in olive oil and then in bread crumb mixture. Preheat broiler to 450° and place breaded chicken breasts on broiler pan 4 inches from element. Broil about 4 minutes on each side or until lightly browned. It is very important you don't overcook. Serve immediately.

Yields 8 servings.

Wine selection: Opitergio Pinot Grigio, a light-bodied dry white

Italian Chicken Breasts

6 boneless, skinless chicken fillets
6 tomatoes, peeled
$\frac{1}{2}$ teaspoon garlic powder
1 teaspoon oregano
$\frac{1}{2}$ teaspoon basil
$\frac{1}{4}$ cup olive oil
1 8-ounce package mozzarella cheese, sliced $\frac{1}{8}$-inch thick
salt and pepper
Parmesan cheese

Pound chicken with flat side of cleaver until flat. Salt and pepper to taste. Heat olive oil and brown chicken about 3 minutes on each side. While chicken is browning, chop up tomatoes in small pieces and put in small saucepan. Let this come to a boil and mix in garlic powder, basil and oregano. Salt and pepper to taste and let cook on low heat 10 minutes. Place browned chicken in shallow casserole dish and cover with mozzarella cheese. Pour drippings from skillet in with the tomato sauce and mix well. Pour tomato sauce over chicken and sprinkle generously with Parmesan cheese. Place under heated broiler 4 minutes or until cheese melts and serve on a warm platter.

Yields 4 servings.

Wine selection: Corvo Rosso, a medium-bodied red

Chicken Casserole with White Sauce

3 cups cooked chicken
4 tablespoons butter
4 tablespoons flour
3 cups chicken broth
2 egg yolks, beaten
1/2 cup cream
1 green pepper, chopped
1 4-ounce can mushrooms, sliced
1 8-ounce package noodles
1/2 cup buttered bread crumbs

Make a white sauce with butter, flour and 3 cups chicken broth. Mix egg yolks and cream together. Pour white sauce over the egg and cream mixture, slowly stirring constantly until smooth and well blended. Boil noodles in water until just tender and drain. Sauté pepper in butter. Mix chicken pieces, green pepper and mushrooms together. Grease casserole dish and sprinkle with 1/2 buttered bread crumbs. Place a layer of noodles and a layer of chicken and white sauce, alternating until all ingredients have been used. Sprinkle the top with remaining bread crumbs and bake 25 minutes in a 375° oven or until bubbly. Serve hot.

Yields 8 servings.

Wine selection: Opitergia Chardonnay, a soft, medium-bodied dry white

Chicken in White Wine with Mushrooms

4 boneless, skinless chicken fillets
4 drumsticks
4 thighs
4 tablespoons olive oil, extra virgin or pure
2/3 cup dry white wine
1/2 pound mushrooms, sliced
1 cup sour cream
1/4 teaspoon flaked red pepper
1 1/2 teaspoons salt
1 teaspoon pepper

Season chicken with salt and pepper and sauté in olive oil until golden brown. Add wine, cover and simmer 30 minutes. Remove chicken and keep warm. Add mushrooms, red pepper and a dash of salt and pepper. Simmer 5 minutes. Stir frequently. Remove from heat. Stir in sour cream and 1/2 teaspoon salt. Return to heat and simmer and stir very gently 2 minutes. To serve, pour sauce over chicken.

Yields 4 servings.

Wine selection: Opitergio Merlot, a young, light-bodied red

Chicken Crab Meat Casserole

3 cups cooked chicken, cut in bite-size pieces
1 6½-ounce can crab meat
1 cup avocado, cubed
1 tablespoon lemon juice
2 medium onions, chopped
1 stick butter
6 tablespoons flour
1 teaspoon salt
1 teaspoon rosemary, crushed
2 cups chicken broth
2 cups sour cream
2 egg yolks
1 cup coarse bread crumbs
2 tablespoons butter

In a saucepan, sauté onions until golden brown. Stir in flour, salt and rosemary. Cook mixture over low heat, stirring constantly, until it bubbles. Beat egg yolks and mix in chicken broth. Gradually add mixture to saucepan, stirring constantly, until the sauce comes to a boil. Remove it from heat and stir in sour cream a little at a time; add chicken meat and crab meat. Sprinkle avocado cubes with lemon juice and blend the mixture gently into the chicken mixture. Pour into 2-quart casserole dish and cover the top evenly with bread crumbs sautéed in butter. Bake in moderate oven at 350° 30 minutes. Serve immediately.

Yields 6 to 8 servings.

Wine selection: White Hall Lane Chenin Blanc, a fruity dry white

Chicken with Smothered Rice

6 boneless, skinless chicken fillets
1 cup flour
1½ cups vegetable oil
2 medium onions, cut crosswise in ⅛-inch thick slices
2 cups water
1 tablespoon distilled white vinegar (optional)
1 cup cooked Minute Rice

Pat the chicken breast completely dry with paper towels and season to taste on both sides with salt and pepper. One at a time dip the pieces in the cup of flour and turn to coat them evenly. Shake each piece to remove excess flour.

Put 1½ cups of oil in a 12-inch skillet at least 2 inches deep, equipped with a heavy lid (an iron skillet preferred). When the oil is very hot, but not smoking, place the pieces of chicken in the skillet and cover. Fry 4 minutes, turn the chicken and still continue to fry, tightly covered, 4 to 5 minutes or until the chicken is evenly browned on both sides. Transfer the chicken to a place that you can keep it warm while you make the onion gravy. Pour off all but 1 tablespoon of fat and sauté onions. Sprinkle them with 2 tablespoons flour and make a roux. Do not scorch. Stirring constantly with a spoon, pour in the water in a slow stream and cook until the gravy comes to a boil, thickens and is smooth. Stir in the vinegar; salt and pepper to taste. Serve over rice covered with gravy.

Yields 5 to 6 servings.

Turkey and Pasta

2 cups cooked turkey, diced
1 cup cooked ham, diced
1 large onion, diced
3 tablespoons olive oil, extra virgin or pure
2 15-ounce cans tomato sauce
$^{1}/_{2}$ cup water
1 teaspoon oregano
$^{1}/_{4}$ teaspoon salt
$^{1}/_{2}$ teaspoon pepper
1 teaspoon garlic powder
1 cup uncooked pasta, broken in $^{1}/_{2}$- to 1-inch lengths

In a 12-inch skillet, brown onion in cooking oil over medium heat. Add remaining ingredients except noodles and blend thoroughly; cover and simmer 10 minutes. Stir in pasta, cover and cook 12 minutes. Stir 2 to 3 times so that noodles will not stick to bottom of skillet. Serve hot with garden peas and a peach half.

Yields 6 to 8 servings.

Wine selection: Mastroberardino Lacrimerosa, a fruity dry red

Turkey Cacciatore

4 cups cooked turkey, cut into short strips
4 cups of your favorite tomato sauce or use *Twenty Minute Tomato Sauce*
1 pound linguine or fettuccine, cooked al dente

Add turkey to tomato sauce and simmer 15 minutes. Toss with pasta. Serve immediately with grated Parmesan or Romano cheese. Goes well with a Caesar salad.

Yields 6 servings.

Wine selection: Sutter Home White Zinfandel, a fruity blush, sweet to dry

Barbecued Turkey Wings

3 turkey wings, disjointed, wing tips discarded
$^{1}/_{3}$ cup cooking oil
$^{1}/_{2}$ stick butter or margarine
2 cups tomato sauce
2 cups barbecue sauce (your favorite)
1 cup water
2 large onions, coarsely chopped
1 cup celery, coarsely diced
1 teaspoon salt
1 teaspoon pepper

Salt and pepper each turkey piece and brown in vegetable oil and set aside. Sauté onion and celery until lightly browned. Add tomato sauce, barbecue sauce, water and salt and pepper. Stir and cook 2 minutes. Arrange turkey wings in a shallow baking dish. Cover with entire amount of sauce. Bake in a preheated oven at 350° 1 hour and 40 minutes, turning occasionally. If sauce gets too thick, add a small amount of water from time to time. Place turkey wings and sauce on a bed of rice.

Yields 6 servings.

Memorial Day Barbecue Chicken

1 3- to 3¹/₂-pound chicken
3 teaspoons butter or margarine
1 medium onion, chopped
2 heaping tablespoons brown sugar
1 teaspoon salt
1 tablespoon Worcestershire sauce
¹/₂ cup water
3 teaspoons vinegar
¹/₂ tablespoon prepared mustard
1 15-ounce can tomato sauce

Cut chicken into serving pieces and brown in hot fat in frying pan; set browned chicken pieces in roasting pan. Brown chopped onions in remaining fat, add the rest of the sauce ingredients and let simmer 10 minutes; pour sauce over chicken and cover pan. Bake in oven at 350° 1 hour or until chicken is tender. Serve sauce over egg noodles or a bed of rice.

Yields 6 servings.

Chicken Breast Kebobs

1¹/₂ pounds boneless, skinless chicken fillets, each cut in half
4 green peppers, cut in 2-inch pieces
1 1-pound can small potatoes
12 small white onions, peeled
1 12-ounce bottle Italian salad dressing
salt and pepper

Salt and pepper chicken pieces and marinate in salad dressing 2 to 3 hours. Salt and pepper onions and green peppers to taste. On a 7-inch skewer, string a piece of chicken, potato, pepper and onion; repeat 3 more times. Place on a grill over medium heat 4 to 6 inches from fire. Brush with remaining liquids and cook 20 to 25 minutes, turning 3 to 4 times. Remove food from each skewer onto a hot plate and serve.

Yields 6 servings.

Chicken and Rib Barbecue Pac

heavy duty aluminum foil, 18 × 25 inches
1/2 cup sauerkraut
2 pieces of a chicken, 1 leg plus 1 thigh or wing
1/2 pound lean spare ribs
1 carrot, cut lengthwise
1 baking potato, cut in quarters, skin left on
4 tablespoons water
your favorite barbecue sauce

Sprinkle meat and vegetables with salt and pepper to taste. Lay aluminum foil on a flat surface and spread sauerkraut in center. Place spare ribs on sauerkraut and spread 3 tablespoons barbecue sauce over ribs. Place chicken skin side up on top of ribs and spread 4 tablespoons barbecue sauce over chicken. Tuck carrots on one side and quartered potato on the other; add 4 tablespoons water and 1 pad of butter. Bring the two opposite edges of foil together over mixture and seal. Place foil pac on a hot grill and cook 1 hour. If grill has a hood close it. You can also use a preheated oven at 375° and cook 1 hour. Serve 1 pac per person with your favorite bread.

Dominick's Special Chicken Barbecue Sauce

1 6-ounce can frozen unsweetened orange juice concentrate
juice of 5 lemons
$1/2$ cup olive oil
$1/2$ cup water
2 cloves garlic, crushed
1 teaspoon salt
$1/2$ teaspoon pepper
$1/2$ teaspoon Accent (MSG)
1 teaspoon oregano

Blend all ingredients thoroughly. Apply generously to chicken 4 to 5 times while barbecuing. This recipe will barbecue 1 to 2 chickens.

Tips on Barbecuing Chicken:

1. Start charcoal fire early and do not use too much charcoal.
2. Allow fire to burn down so that coals are covered with a white ash.
3. Keep chicken 6 inches above fire.
4. Cut up chicken either in halves or quarters or serving pieces.
5. Remove wings and barbecue separately.
6. Cut halfway through thigh and leg joints.
7. Lightly salt chicken on both sides.
8. Lightly oil the grill and place chicken on it, skin side up.
9. Turn chicken frequently and apply barbecue sauce generously.
10. Allow at least 1 to $1 1/4$ hours for cooking time, depending on size.

Mabel's Improved Chicken Barbecue Sauce

1 6-ounce can frozen lemonade concentrate
1 6-ounce can frozen orange juice concentrate
3 ounces wine vinegar
1 teaspoon garlic powder
1 rounded tablespoon oregano
$1/2$ teaspoon pepper or to taste
1 teaspoon salt or to taste
4 ounces olive oil, extra virgin or pure

Thaw lemonade and orange juice concentrate and blend with remaining ingredients. Marinate 1 $3^{1}/_{2}$- to 4-pound chicken 2 hours or overnight and then barbecue. Apply sauce generously while barbecuing.

Seafood

Pappa Rosario's Piscestocco

3³/₄-inch dried codfish steaks or any other firm-fleshed fish, soaked in clean water for 36 hours
   or 2 pounds fresh codfish steaks, cut in 2-inch pieces
2 cups tomatoes, chopped coarse
1 large yellow onion, chopped coarse
3 tablespoons green salad olives, rinsed
1 tablespoon dried oregano
salt and pepper to taste
¹/₂ teaspoon flaked red pepper
2 tablespoons olive oil, extra virgin or pure
1 large bell pepper, sliced thin
1 carrot, sliced thin
1 cup celery, cut in ¹/₂-inch pieces
4 cloves garlic, chopped coarse
1 pound cooked pasta of your choice

In a 6-quart saucepan, brown onions in olive oil. Add remaining ingredients except fish and bell pepper. Bring to a boil and simmer 30 minutes. Add bell pepper. Cook 10 minutes, then add codfish and simmer covered an additional 15 minutes. Serve over the cooked pasta.

Yields 8 servings.

Wine selection: Robert Montavi Cabernet Sauvignon, a rich dry red

Sicilian Pasta con Sarde

1¹/₂ pounds sardines, cleaned and deboned (may substitute flounder fillets)
2 medium onions, sliced thin
¹/₂ cup pine nuts or chopped walnuts
¹/₂ cup pure olive oil or more if needed
6 flat anchovies, chopped fine
3 cloves garlic, minced
1 fennel bulb, cut in 8 pieces and cooked or 1 small stalk of celery plus 1 tablespoon fennel seed, cut in 3-inch pieces and cooked (instructions below)
salt and pepper to taste

Divide fish into 2 equal portions. Sauté onions in oil in a large skillet 5 to 7 minutes. Add ¹/₂ of fish to onions and cook. With a wooden spoon, break up fish into small pieces and continue cooking 5 minutes. Add anchovy, garlic, nuts and chopped fennel or celery and ¹/₂ cup reserve liquid. Cook 3 minutes. Set aside. Sauté remaining whole fish fillets in oil and drain on paper towels. Keep warm. Cook 1 pound of tubular pasta in reserved liquid (4 quarts) al dente. Drain. Mix pasta with ¹/₂ sardine sauce. In a 9 × 12 × 2 pan, cover bottom with ¹/₃ pasta. Top with 6 to 8 cooked sardine fillets covered with ¹/₃ cup sauce. Repeat until all ingredients are used up. Top layer should have 6 to 8 sardine fillets and some sauce. Preheat oven to 375°. Bake 20 minutes. Let stand 5 minutes and serve.

Cooking instructions for fennel/celery:

To 4¹/₂ quarts salted, boiling water, add the cut up fennel or celery. If celery is used, add 1 tablespoon fennel seed wrapped in cheese cloth; discard after cooking. Cook 20 minutes. Remove with a slotted spoon, cool and chop coarse. Reserve liquid.

Yields 8 servings.

Wine selection: Corvo, a medium-bodied dry white

Steamed Mussels with Garlic and Wine

2- to 2¹/₂-pounds mussels, scrubbed and washed
¹/₄ cup fresh parsley, chopped coarse
1 cup dry white wine
4 to 5 cloves garlic, chopped coarse
3 tablespoons olive oil, extra virgin or pure
2 tablespoons lemon juice

Place washed mussels in a large pan with a tight cover. Add the parsley, garlic, wine and lemon juice. Toss gently with a wooden spoon until all the mussels are coated. Sprinkle olive oil over mussels and cover. Heat to a boil; reduce heat and steam 10 minutes. Makes a great appetizer. Juices may be spooned over toasted Italian bread and sprinkled with Parmesan cheese for an additional treat.

Wine selection: BV Sauvignon Blanc, a crisp dry white

Stuffed Calamari

1¹/₂ pounds squid
2 cloves garlic, minced
4 anchovy flats, minced
2 tablespoons parsley, chopped fine
2 large eggs, beaten
salt and pepper to taste
¹/₂ cup bread crumbs, dried
2 tablespoons olive oil, extra virgin or pure

Wash and skin squid; remove ink sack and cartilage and discard. Chop tentacles as fine as possible and mix with garlic, anchovies and parsley. Mix breadcrumbs, eggs and olive oil; salt and pepper to taste. Add the anchovy and tentacle mix and blend. Stuff the mix into squid and clamp ends with round toothpick. Season with salt and pepper. Broil 4 to 5 inches from heat 7 to 8 minutes on each side. Brush with olive oil before turning. Serve with lemon wedges. Makes an excellent appetizer or a great meal with pasta and white sauce.

Yields 6 servings.

Wine selection: Macrina Verdicchio, a tart, crisp dry white

Sautéed Flounder Fillets

4 flounder fillets (may substitute sole, catfish or turbo)
1 large egg, beaten in ¼ cup milk
salt and pepper to taste
seasoned salt
¼ cup pure olive oil

Breading:

⅓ cup Parmesan cheese
⅔ cup dry bread crumbs
1 teaspoon garlic powder
2 tablespoons parsley, minced

Season flounder fillets to taste. Dip in egg mix and then coat with crumb mix. Shake off excess. In a heavy nonstick skillet over medium heat, add oil and sauté fish gently until lightly brown. Turn and cook an additional 2 to 3 minutes. Drain on paper towels and keep warm. Serve with an Italian veggie frittata and a fresh lettuce and onion salad.

Yields 4 servings.

Wine selection: Centine Bianco, a dry white with a touch of spritziness

Baked Fish/Onions

1- to 1¼-pounds fish steaks, ¾-inch thick (may substitute halibut, cod or tuna)
salt and pepper to taste
1 yellow onion, sliced thin
1 bunch green onions, cut in ½-inch pieces, include some tails
1 cup mushrooms, sliced
2 tablespoons pure olive oil
½ cup dry white wine or chicken broth

Preheat oven to 425°. Sauté onions and mushrooms in olive oil over medium-high heat until wilted. Meanwhile, salt and pepper fish. In a baking pan, place ½ of sautéed onion mix in bottom of pan. Add fish, then top with remaining onion mix. Add wine or broth. Bake 12 to 15 minutes or until fish flakes off easily with fork; do not cover. Serve with carrots and zucchini for a healthy lowcal meal.

Yields 4 servings.

Wine selection: Robert Mondavi Pinot Noir, a fruity, medium-bodied dry red

Spicy Fish Fillets

6 4- to 5-ounce fish fillets (trout, flounder, catfish or sole)
salt and pepper to taste
$^{1}/_{4}$ cup pure olive oil, divided

Sauce:
1 bunch green onions, cut in $^{1}/_{2}$-inch pieces, include some tails
2 cloves garlic, chopped coarse
1 large tomato, chopped coarse
$^{2}/_{3}$ cup green peas, fresh or frozen
$^{2}/_{3}$ cup yellow squash, cut in $^{1}/_{2}$-inch cubes
3 tablespoons parsley, chopped coarse
$^{1}/_{2}$ teaspoon flaked red pepper or to taste
salt and pepper to taste
1 tablespoon wine vinegar
$^{1}/_{4}$ cup milk, mixed with 2 tablespoons flour

Sauté fish fillets in $^{1}/_{2}$ of olive oil. Drain on paper towels. Keep warm. Sauté green onions until golden brown and limp. Add garlic, parsley, tomato, squash, peas, red pepper, vinegar, salt and pepper. Cook over medium-high heat 3 to 4 minutes. Stir in milk with flour and cook until slightly thickened. Top each fillet with sauce. Serve with pasta and red sauce.

Yields 6 servings.

Wine selection: BV Cabernet Sauvignon, a fruity, medium-bodied dry red

Poached Swordfish Steaks

4 4- to 6-ounce fresh swordfish steaks, ³/₄-inch thick
³/₄ cup dry white wine
2 slices fresh lemon plus 1 teaspoon juice
1 teaspoon oregano
2 tablespoons fresh parsley, chopped coarse
³/₄ cup chicken stock, fresh or canned
2 tablespoons capers
¹/₂ cup half-and-half (for variation add 1 tablespoon pesto sauce)
salt and pepper to taste

Combine wine, chicken stock, lemon slices and oregano in a heavy skillet. Bring to a boil. Salt and pepper fish to taste and place in a skillet. Cover tightly and poach fish steaks slowly over low heat 7 to 8 minutes. Remove fish to a warm platter. Increase heat and boil liquids 5 minutes or until reduced by ¹/₃. Remove lemon slices, lower heat, add cream, capers, lemon juice and parsley. Season to taste. Stir frequently, cooking an additional 3 minutes. Pour over fish steaks and serve. Goes well with boiled potatoes and steamed broccoli.

Yields 4 servings.

Wine selection: Fetzer Sundial Chardonnay, a fruity dry white

Rice and Shrimp

1 16-ounce can tomatoes, crushed
2 cups long grain rice
6 cups chicken broth, fresh or canned
salt and pepper to taste
1 pound shelled shrimp
1 10-ounce package frozen okra, sliced
2 cups celery, cut in 1/2-inch pieces
1/2 cup parsley, chopped coarse
1 medium yellow or red bell pepper, chopped coarse
1 bunch spinach, trimmed and torn into pieces
1 teapsoon flaked red pepper (less if desired)
1 1/2 tablespoons oregano
3 cloves garlic, chopped coarse or 1 teaspoon garlic powder
1 large yellow onion, sliced thin
1/4 cup olive or vegetable oil

In a large stew pot, sauté onions in oil. Add remaining ingredients except rice and shrimp. Bring to a boil. Adjust seasoning to taste. Cover and simmer 30 minutes. Add rice and cook 10 minutes. Add shrimp and cook an additional 10 minutes. Turn heat off and let stand 10 minutes. Serve in soup bowls with crusty Italian or French bread.

Yields 12 servings.

Wine selection: White Hall Lane Chenin Blanc, a dry white

Sicilian Calamari

2 pounds fresh squid, cleaned and cut in 1-inch pieces, tentacles included
2½ pounds tomatoes, chopped coarse
1 15-ounce can tomato sauce
1 large onion, sliced thin
1½ cups fresh celery, cut in 1-inch pieces
1 green bell pepper, cut in strips
¼ cup fresh parsley, chopped coarse
1 tablespoon oregano
1½ cups mushrooms, sliced
4 cloves garlic, minced
salt and pepper to taste
½ teaspoon red flaked pepper or to taste
¼ cup pure olive oil

In a heavy sauce pan, sauté onions and celery 7 to 8 minutes. Add tomatoes and sauce, garlic, parsley, oregano, red pepper and salt and pepper to taste. Simmer over low heat 20 minutes. Add squid, green pepper and mushrooms and cook an additional 15 minutes. Meanwhile, cook 1 pound of your favorite pasta al dente and serve squid over the pasta.

Yields 6 servings.

Wine selection: Claiborne and Churchill Gewurztraminer, a crisp dry white

Swordfish di Santo

4 6-ounce swordfish steaks ³/₄-inch thick
2 medium yellow onions, sliced thin
2 tablespoons wine vinegar
¹/₄ cup fresh parsley, chopped
¹/₂ teaspoon dried oregano
¹/₂ teaspoon basil
¹/₂ cup wine
pure olive oil

Wash fish and dry on paper towels. Season with salt and pepper; set aside. In a heavy skillet, add 3 tablespoons olive oil. Over medium-high heat, sauté onions 4 to 5 minutes. Add vinegar, parsley, oregano and basil. Stir until well blended and continue cooking until onions are limp and all liquid is cooked out. Drain onions on paper towels. Preheat oven to 375°. In a baking pan, cover bottom with olive oil. Arrange fish in one layer. Add wine. Bake 8 to 10 minutes. Baste 2 to 3 times. Top each steak with onion mix. Bake 5 minutes or until fish flakes easily. Goes well with pasta and white sauce.

Yields 4 servings.

Wine selection: Inglenook Niebaum Claret, a medium-bodied dry red

Poached Salmon Steaks

6 4- to 6-ounce salmon steaks, ³/4-inch thick, salt and pepper to taste
1 cup white wine (Johannisberg Riesling)
1 cup water
2 tablespoons lemon juice
1 bay leaf

In a large frying pan with cover, combine all ingredients except fish. Bring to a boil; add fish in one layer, reduce heat and simmer covered 7 to 8 minutes or until fish flakes easily. Remove to a warm platter and garnish with chopped fresh parsley. Serve with boiled potatoes and a fresh green salad. Excellent lowcal dish.

Yields 6 servings.

Wine selection: Chateau St. Michel, a fruity white

Sicilian Oyster and Artichoke Stew

1 14-ounce can artichoke hearts, chopped coarse

1 10-ounce jar fresh shucked oysters, cut in half, retain juice

2 cups white potatoes, cubed

$1/4$ cup olive oil, pure or extra virgin

2 bunches green onions, cut in $1/2$-inch pieces, include some tails

3 cloves fresh garlic, minced or 1 teaspoon garlic powder

2 teaspoons oregano

2 bay leaves

3 cups chicken broth, fresh or canned

$1/2$ to 1 teaspoon flaked red pepper

$1/2$ cup dry white wine

2 teaspoons Worcestershire sauce

Sauté onions in olive oil in a 6-quart sauce pan. Add chicken broth, potatoes, onions, artichokes and seasonings. Simmer 15 minutes. Add oysters with juice and remaining ingredients. Adjust salt and pepper, simmer 10 minutes covered. Discard bay leaves. Serve with hard-crusted Italian bread or French bread in large soup bowls.

Yields 6 to 8 servings.

Wine selection: Bricco Viole Sebaste, a fruity, medium-bodied dry red

White Sauce II

¼ cup extra virgin olive oil
½ cup Parmesan cheese plus 1 tablespoon flour, blended
2 cups half-and-half or skim milk
1 teaspoon pepper
1 teaspoon garlic powder
2 tablespoons fresh parsley, chopped medium coarse

In a large frying pan over medium heat, make a roux with cheese mix and olive oil; stir constantly until bubbly, do not brown. Add the cream or milk plus parsley and heat until the sauce thickens slightly. Stir in the sautéed shrimp and toss with pasta. Use a large frying pan that will hold the sauce, shrimp and pasta. Sauté shrimp first, then use the same pan to make your white sauce. Serve out of frying pan. Pasta and shrimp must be kept hot.

Wine selection: Villa Banfi Chardonnay, a medium-bodied dry white

Broiled Breaded Catfish Rolls

2 whole catfish fillets, cut in half
vegetable oil

Breading:

⅔ cup dry bread crumbs
⅓ Parmesan cheese
1 teaspoon garlic powder
½ teaspoon pepper
2 tablespoons parsley, chopped fine

Salt and pepper catfish to taste. Brush or dip in vegetable oil, then coat with breading (about ½ cup). Roll each piece like a jelly roll and secure with toothpicks. Broil 5 to 6 inches below heat 3 minutes or until brown, then turn and broil an additional 3 minutes.

Yields 4 servings.

Italian Catfish

2 whole catfish fillets, cut in half
1 15-ounce can whole tomatoes
1 medium onion, sliced thin
1 rounded teaspoon oregano
$^1/_2$ teaspoon garlic powder
$^3/_4$ teaspoon salt
$^1/_2$ teaspoon pepper
3 tablespoons vegetable oil

Salt and pepper catfish to taste. Sauté onions in oil in an 8-inch frying pan until lightly browned. Crush tomatoes and add to onions. Stir in salt, pepper, garlic powder and oregano. Simmer uncovered 5 mintues. Add catfish and spoon the sauce over fillets. Cover and simmer 7 minutes. Serve over cooked fettuccine.

Yields 4 servings.

Wine selection: Antinori Castello della Sala or Orvietto Classico, crisp dry whites

Catfish in Tomato Sauce

1 pound catfish strips or nuggets
1 16-ounce can tomato sauce
1 16-ounce can tomatoes, crushed
1 large yellow onion, sliced thin
$1^1/_2$ teaspoons dried basil
1 teaspoon garlic powder
1 teaspoon salt
$^3/_4$ teaspoon black pepper
$^1/_4$ cup vegetable oil

In a heavy skillet, lightly brown catfish in oil. Drain on paper towels. In same skillet, sauté onions until golden color. Add remaining ingredients, bring to a slow boil and adjust seasonings to taste. Stir and cook uncovered 15 minutes. Add catfish and cook 5 minutes. Meanwhile, cook 1 pound of linguine al dente until tender, drain and toss with the catfish sauce.

Yields 6 servings.

Wine selection: Fontana Candida Frascati, a soft dry white

Catfish Frittata

1 pound catfish strips or nuggets
1 large bell pepper, cut in 1-inch strips
2 large tomatoes, chopped coarse
1 large yellow onion, sliced thin
6 ounces mushrooms, sliced
2 tablespoons fresh parsley, chopped
1 teaspoon garlic powder
¹/₂ teaspoon black pepper
2 teaspoons salt
¹/₄ cup vegetable oil

In a large skillet, sauté onions in oil 2 to 3 minutes over medium-high heat. Add bell pepper and mushrooms and cook 3 to 4 minutes. Add tomatoes, seasonings and catfish, stir, bring to a slow boil and reduce heat. Adjust seasonings to taste. Cook 8 minutes or until fish flakes with a fork. Serve over cooked rice.

Yields 6 servings.

Wine selection: Boscaini Pinot Grigio, a tart, crisp dry white

Broiled Whole Catfish

4 whole catfish, ²/₃- to ³/₄-pound each
salt and pepper or seasoned salt to taste

Breading:
²/₃ cup dried bread crumbs
1 teaspoon garlic powder
¹/₃ cup Parmesan cheese
2 tablespoons parsley, chopped
olive oil or vegetable oil

Preheat broiler 450°. Wash catfish in cold water. Dry with paper towels. Make 2 slashes on each side, about 1 inch apart, on the thickest part of the fish. Brush generously with oil and season with salt and pepper or seasoned salt. Roll in bread crumb mixture, including body cavity. Line broiler pan with aluminum foil. Brush with oil and place pan 4 inches below heat. Arrange catfish in middle of pan and broil 6 minutes. Turn and broil an additional 6 minutes. Remove with a spatula and serve with your favorite vegetables.

Yields 4 servings.

Wine selection: Gancia Brut, dry, crisp, sparkling

Baked Catfish with Onions and Tomatoes

4 whole catfish, 2/3- to 3/4-pound each
salt and pepper or seasoned salt to taste
1/4 cup parsley, chopped coarse
2 large tomatoes or 1 16-ounce can tomatoes, crushed
2 bunches green onions, cut in 1-inch pieces including tails
3 cloves garlic, minced
2 tablespoons oregano
1/2 teaspoon flaked red pepper

Preheat oven to 400°. Wash catfish, do not dry. Make 2 slashes on each side, about 1 inch apart, on the thickest part of the fish. Brush generously with oil and season with salt and pepper or seasoned salt. Set fish aside. In a mixing bowl, combine crushed tomatoes, onions, parsley, red pepper, garlic, oregano and 2 tablespoons oil; mix. Season to taste. In a 9 × 12 × 2-inch baking pan, cover bottom with 1/2 cup tomato and onion mix. Arrange fish in pan, then pour remainder of sauce over fish. Bake in preheated oven 25 to 30 minutes or until fish flakes easily with a fork. Serve fish with pasta or rice.

Yields 4 servings.

Wine selection: Robert Mondavi Fume Blanc, a dry white

Shrimp di Dominic

1 pound medium shrimp, shelled, deveined, washed and drained on paper towels
3 tablespoons fresh parsley, chopped coarse
salt and pepper to taste
4 cloves fresh garlic, minced
1 cup seasoned bread crumbs
1/2 cup Parmesan cheese, grated
1/3 cup pure olive oil

Preheat broiler 450°. Cover bottom of 9 × 12 × 2-inch baking pan with 1/2 cup bread crumbs. Arrange shrimp over bread crumbs in rows. Salt and pepper. Sprinkle evenly with garlic, cheese and parsley. Top with remaining bread crumbs. Drizzle olive oil over crumbs and place pan under broiler about 5 inches from heat. Broil 7 to 8 minutes. Shrimp will turn orange in color. Watch closely. If bread crumbs get too brown, lower heat to 400°. Serve with pasta and **White** *or* **Pesto Sauce.**

Yields 4 servings.

Wine selection: Simi Chardonnay, a rich, full-bodied dry white

Seafood/Dijon Mustard

6 5- to 6-ounce salmon steaks, ³/₄-inch thick or other firm fish steaks

Mustard sauce:

3 tablespoons Dijon mustard
3 tablespoons onion, minced
3 tablespoons fresh lemon juice
¹/₃ cup pure olive oil

Combine in a mixing bowl. Blend with wire whisk. Preheat oven to 375°. Brush baking pan with olive oil. Dip fish steaks in mustard sauce on both sides and arrange in baking pan. Bake 20 minutes or until fish flakes easily with a fork (check after 15 minutes).

To Grill:

Over high heat, grill 5 to 6 minutes on each side. Baste with sauce. When fish flakes easily it is done. Garnish with chopped parsley and serve.

For whole catfish:

Make 2 slashes on each thick part of catfish. Cover with mustard sauce. Bake same as above.

Yields 6 servings.

Wine selection: Kendall Jackson Chardonnay, a medium-bodied dry white

Scampi Siciliano Al Furno

1 1/2 pounds fresh medium or large shrimp, shelled, deveined, cleaned, and drained on paper
   towels
salt and pepper to taste
1/4 cup olive oil, extra virgin or pure
2 tablespoons olive oil

Breading:

1/3 cup Parmesan cheese, grated
2/3 cup dry bread crumbs
1 teaspoon garlic powder
1/4 teaspoon flaked red pepper (optional)

*In a mixing bowl, blend all ingredients. Preheat oven to 400°. Place shrimp in a mixing
bowl. Pour 1/4 cup oil over shrimp and blend making sure all shrimp are well coated with
oil. Add coated shrimp to bowl containing breading mix and coat evenly. Do not shake off
excess breading. Coat bottom of 9 × 12 × 2-inch baking pan with 2 tablespoons oil. Add
shrimp and distribute evenly in pan. Bake 20 minutes. Shrimp will turn an orange-red.
Serve with linguine and **Pesto Sauce** or **White Sauce.***

Yields 4 to 6 servings.

Wine selection: Sutter White Zinfandel, a soft, sweet blush

Special Main Courses

Chicken Cacciatore

1 3- to 3½-pound chicken, cut in serving pieces
salt and pepper to taste
1 bell pepper, cut in ½-inch strips
1 cup mushrooms, sliced
Quickie Twenty Minute Sauce

Salt and pepper each piece. Brown in olive oil. Place chicken in sauce and simmer 45 minutes, covered. Last 10 minutes add bell pepper and mushrooms; salt and pepper to taste. Blend into sauce, cover and complete cooking. Pasta may be served with remaing sauce.

Yields 6 servings.

Wine selection: Gattinara, a medium to full-bodied dry red

Chicken Cacciatore II

2 pounds boneless, skinless chicken fillets, cut into bite-size nuggets
salt and pepper or seasoned salt to taste
4 cups *Fresh Tomato Sauce I*
1 large bell pepper, cut in chunks
1 cup mushrooms, sliced

Salt and pepper chicken breast and lightly sauté in 3 tablespoons olive oil. Add fillets to tomato sauce and bring to a slow boil and simmer 15 minutes. Sauté peppers and mushrooms and add to sauce; cook 5 minutes. (Can also be baked in a 375° degree oven 45 minutes.) Cook 1 pound of your favorite pasta al dente and drain. Place on warm plates. Pour sauce and chicken over pasta. Sprinkle with Parmesan cheese and serve immediately.

Yields 6 servings.

Wine selection: Brunello di Montalcino, a full-bodied dry red

BBQ Italian Beef Brisket

1 8- to 10-pound beef brisket (packer trim), fat trimmed off
1 bunch fresh parsley
8 to 10 fresh cloves of garlic, peeled and cut in half
seasoned salt or salt and pepper
1/4 cup pure olive oil

Wash brisket under cold water and pat dry. Pinch off 1 cup of parsley leaves; discard stems. Place brisket on a work surface fat side up. With a sharp knife, pierce meat about 1 inch deep, make a good size hole and insert 1 piece of garlic and some parsley leaves. Repeat over entire surface of brisket, placing inserts 2 to 3 inches apart. Be sure garlic and parsley are inserted fully into meat. Sprinkle generously with seasoned salt on both sides, wrap in foil and marinate in refrigerator overnight. Preheat oven to 300°. Place brisket in roasting pan, drizzle oil over meat, cover with foil and cook 4 hours. Cool; trim excess fat. Put brisket on a cutting board and slice. Serve with natural gravy; decant fat.

Yields 15 to 20 servings.

Wine selection: BV Cabernet Sauvignon Rutherford, a dry red

Italian Veal Cutlets

1 pound veal cutlets, 1/4-inch thick
2 large eggs, mixed with 2 tablespoons water and beaten
1/4 cup olive oil
salt and pepper

Breading:

2/3 cup dry bread crumbs
1/3 cup Parmesan cheese, grated
1 teaspoon garlic powder
2 tablespoons parsley, chopped coarse

Pound veal to tenderize and sprinkle with salt and pepper. Dip in egg mixture and then coat with breading. In a heavy, non-stick skillet, heat olive oil over medium heat. Gently sauté veal until lightly brown, 2 to 3 minutes on each side. Serve with pasta and salad.

Yields 4 servings.

Wine selection: Corvo, a smooth and fruity white

Stuffed Veal Chops—Sicilian Style

6 loin veal chops, cut 1-inch thick with a pocket in each

Stuffing:

$\frac{1}{2}$ cup bread crumbs
$\frac{1}{4}$ pound prosciuto (Italian ham), chopped coarse
2 ounces mozarella, shredded
2 ounces Parmesan cheese, grated
4 ounces mushrooms, minced
$\frac{1}{4}$ cup parsley, minced
$\frac{1}{2}$ cup dry white wine
salt and pepper to taste
pure olive oil

Preheat oven to 375°. Combine all ingredients except oil. Mix and set aside. Salt and pepper chops including inside pocket. Let stand a few minutes. Brush each chop with olive oil. With your fingers, fill each pocket with stuffing and secure opening with a toothpick. Brush baking pan with oil and arrange chops on bottom. Bake 45 minutes. Remove from oven, cover with foil and let stand 10 minutes. Serve with pasta al pesto or pasta with a fresh tomato sauce.

Yields 6 servings.

Wine selection: Fiano di Avellino, a dry white

Veal Scallopini/Sicilian Style

1 pound veal cutlets, sliced thin
1 large egg, beaten with 2 tablespoons milk and salt and pepper

Breading:

1/3 cup Parmesan cheese
2/3 cup dry bread crumbs
2 tablespoons fresh parsley, chopped medium
1 teaspoon garlic powder
1/4 cup pure olive oil

Gently pound each cutlet with a wooden mallet until it is even thickness of 1/8- to 1/4-inch thick. Lightly salt and pepper. Dip each cutlet in egg mix, shake off excess and coat with bread crumb mix. Set aside until all the cutlets are coated. In a heavy non-stick skillet, add oil over medium heat and sauté each cutlet until golden brown. Drain on paper towels. Serve with your favorite pasta with red tomato or pesto sauce.

Yields 4 to 5 servings.

Wine selection: Castello della Sala (Antinori Sauvignon Blanc), a dry white

Roast Leg of Lamb Sicilian Style

1 6- to 7-pound leg of lamb, boned out
salt and pepper to taste
¼ cup fresh parsley, chopped coarse
2 tablespoons fresh mint, chopped coarse
2 tablespoons fresh basil, chopped coarse or 1½ teaspoons dry
1 teaspoon dry rosemary, crushed
6 large cloves garlic, chopped medium
pure olive oil

Preheat oven to 325°. Place lamb on a large cutting board so it will lay flat. You may have to make some cuts in the thick part of leg. Have some strong cord available to tie leg of lamb. Salt and pepper lamb to taste. Sprinkle with olive oil. Combine parsley, mint, basil and rosemary in a small bowl and blend by hand; sprinkle mix evenly on lamb. Press into meat. Spread garlic evenly over meat and sprinkle with more olive oil. Starting at small end of the leg of lamb, begin rolling meat as in a jelly roll. Tuck in any loose meat and keep the roll tight. When roll is complete have someone help you tie the roll in about 4 or 5 places to secure the roll. Place lamb in roasting pan on a rack. Brush with olive oil and salt and pepper to taste. For medium-well lamb, cook 2½ hours. Remove from oven and let stand 10 minutes. Slice lamb and place on a platter garnished with fresh mint leaves. Goes well with sautéed carrots and zucchini or peas or green beans.

Yields 15 to 20 servings.

Wine selection: Barbaresco, a full-bodied red

Chicken Spedini

2 pounds boneless, skinless chicken fillets or veal cutlets
olive oil, extra virgin or pure
8 bay leaves
24 round toothpicks or more, depends on number of breast pieces

Breading:

2/3 cup dry bread crumbs
1/3 cup Parmesan cheese, grated
1 teaspoon garlic powder
2 tablespoons parsley, chopped coarse

Set oven on broil at 450° to 500°. Cut each fillet in half and pound between wax paper 1/8- to 1/4-inch thick; salt and pepper. Coat each piece of breast meat with olive oil, then with breading. Roll each up tightly. Between 2 rolled up pieces, place 1 bay leaf, then secure with 3 toothpicks. Be sure meat and bay leaf are firmly together. Repeat until all the rolled up pieces are secured. Place on broiler pan, which has been covered with foil, 4 inches from heat and broil 4 minutes on each side. Serve with your favorite pasta.

Yields 8 servings.

Wine selection: Villa Antinari Galestro, a fruity, spritzy, light-bodied white

Sicilian Chicken

6 boneless, skinless chicken breast fillets
1 large yellow onion, sliced thin
8 ounces fresh mushrooms, sliced thin
1/4 cup parsley, chopped coarse
1/2 cup olive oil

Breading:

2/3 cup dry bread crumbs
1/3 cup Parmesan cheese, grated
1 teaspoon garlic powder
2 tablespoons parsley, chopped coarse

Preheat oven to 400°. Season chicken with salt and pepper or seasoned salt. Pour some olive oil into a plate and coat each piece of chicken on both sides; coat with bread crumbs. Lay the chicken with the cut side up on a work counter. Sauté onions, mushrooms and parsley in olive oil 5 to 7 minutes or until onions are limp. Divide into 6 portions and spread on top of each piece of chicken. Tuck the chicken around the filling and turn it over and place it in a baking pan brushed with olive oil; drizzle oil over chicken and bake 25 minutes. Remove with a spatula and serve with mixed fresh veggies.

Yields 6 servings.

Wine selection: Lacryma Christi, a medium-bodied dry white

Quick Grilled Chicken Breasts

4 boneless, skinless chicken fillets, seasoned with salt and pepper or seasoned salt
1/4 cup pure olive oil
1 quart-size ZipLoc bag

*Preheat gas grill or broiler to 500° or charcoal fire. Place chicken in ZipLoc bag. Add olive oil and seal. Rotate bag so chicken is completely coated with oil. Let stand 30 minutes. May be prepared night before; refrigerate. Grill 3 to 4 minutes on each side. Serve right off the grill with a hearty **Sicilian Tomato and Onion Salad**.*

Wine selection: Pinot Grigio, a crisp, fragrant dry white

Quick Italian Roast Chicken

2 18- to 20-ounce cornish hens, cut in half, washed, patted dry and seasoned with salt and pepper or seasoned salt
1 recipe of *Sicilian Basting Sauce II*

Preheat broiler to 475° or 500°. Cover broiling pan with foil. Remove wing tip at second joint; cut through ¹/₂ wing joint at breast. Cut through ¹/₂ leg and thigh joint of each hen. Marinate in basting sauce 4 hours or overnight. Place hens on broiler pan skin side up 4 inches from heat. Broil about 10 minutes, basting several times. Turn and cook additional 10 minutes; baste. Hens should be a golden brown. Pierce thigh for doneness; if liquid is not clear, broil an additional 5 minutes at 450°. Serve with asparagus spears and a garden salad.

To Bake:

Preheat oven to 400°. Place hens in 1 layer in baking pan. Top with ¹/₂ cup basting sauce and bake 30 minutes.

To Grill:

Set gas grill on high, charcoal on hot, about 4 to 5 inches from heat. Grill 7 to 8 minutes on each side; baste frequently. Hens should be a nice golden brown. If necessary, cook an additional minute or two.

Yields 4 servings.

Wine selection: Pinot Bianco, a crisp dry white

Chicken and Artichoke Hearts

3 cups cooked chicken, cubed

2 cups chicken broth

1 14-ounce can artichoke hearts, quartered and drained

1 cup Parmesan cheese, grated

1 large yellow onion, chopped coarse

2 tablespoons olive oil, extra virgin or pure

2 large fresh eggs, beaten

1/4 cup parsley, chopped coarse

3 large cloves garlic, chopped fine

1/2 teaspoon pepper

salt to taste

1 4-ounce jar pimentos, chopped coarse

1/2 teaspoon flaked red pepper, more if desired

3/4 teaspoon rosemary leaves, crushed

1 teaspoon oregano

Preheat oven to 350°. Lightly brown onions in olive oil, retain. In a large mixing bowl, blend eggs, broth, spices, parsley, cheese and onions. Add remaning ingredients and blend thoroughly. Pour mixture into a lightly greased 9 × 12 × 2-inch pan and bake 40 minutes. Serve piping hot over rice. Use remaining broth for egg drop soup.

Yields 8 servings.

Wine selection: California Inglenook Savignon Blanc, a dry white

Chicken Braccioli

2 pounds boneless, skinless chicken fillets, pounded to ¼-inch thickness between wax paper
(may substitute veal cutlets or eye of round)
Quickie Twenty Minute Sauce

Filling:

½ pound Italian sausage, remove from casing
2 hard-boiled eggs, chopped coarse
3 cloves garlic, chopped fine
3 tablespoons parsley, chopped coarse
½ teaspoon flaked red pepper
1 teaspoon oregano
½ cup dry white wine
salt and pepper to taste
toothpicks

*In a mixing bowl, blend all ingredients in filling. Spread the mixture equally on each fillet.
Roll up tightly and secure with 3 toothpicks. Brown lightly in olive oil. Simmer Braccioli
covered in sauce 30 minutes. Pasta may be served with remaining sauce.*

Yields 4 to 8 servings.

Wine selection: California Gallo Red Burgundy, medium-bodied, dry

Beef Braccioli

1½- to 2-pound beef rump roast, cut in ¼-inch slices
1 large onion, sliced thin
8-ounce package mushrooms, sliced thin
3 ounces mozarella cheese, shredded
3 ounces Parmesan cheese, grated
3 cloves garlic, minced
¼ cup fresh parsley, chopped medium
½ cup dry bread crumbs
½ cup pure olive oil, divided
½ pound Italian sausage, remove casing and crumble
salt and pepper to taste
Fresh Tomato Sauce I

With a wooden mallet, gently pound each slice of beef and tenderize. Season with salt and pepper or seasoned salt. Sauté onions in ¼ cup olive oil 5 minutes. In a mixing bowl, add rest of ingredients and mix. Add sautéed onions and mix. Place a thin layer of mix on each slice of beef. Roll up like a jelly roll and secure with 2 toothpicks. Lightly brown in ¼ cup olive oil. Cook in tomato sauce 1 hour. Serve with pasta.

Yields 12 to 14 Braccioli.

Wine selection: Gallo Red Burgundy, medium-bodied, dry

Famous Formica Fried Egg Sandwich

6 large eggs
18 strips lean bacon
6⅛-inch slices red Italian onion
6¼-inch slices tomato
6 romaine lettuce leaves
12 slices whole wheat bread, toasted
mustard
mayonnaise
salt and pepper

Fry bacon crisp on 1 side. Drain on paper towels. Discard fat in pan. Return bacon to frying pan 6 slices at a time, cooked side up. Arrange bacon in 3 slice groups with small space between slices and cook over medium heat. Immediately break 1 egg in the middle of each 3 slice group and let it spread. When eggs solidify, flip over for about 1 minute. Remove from pan and drain on paper towels. Repeat until all eggs are cooked. Meanwhile, spread mayonnaise on 1 slice of bread and mustard on the other. Layer egg and bacon, tomato, onion and lettuce. Salt and pepper to taste. Cut in half and serve with soup or salad for a great meal.

Yields 6 servings.

The Ultimate Chicken Sandwich

4 boneless, skinless chicken breast fillets
4 kaiser rolls, cut in half
olive oil, pure or extra virgin
seasoned salt
2 large yellow onions, sliced thin
4 ounces mozzarella cheese, shredded
2 ounces Parmesan cheese, grated
8 thin slices tomatoes

Gently pound each breast piece with a mallet to a uniform thickness. Brush with olive oil and sprinkle with seasoned salt. Over medium-high heat, sauté breast pieces in small amount of olive oil 1½ to 2 minutes on each side. Drain on paper towels. In same pan, add some olive oil and sauté onions until limp and barely brown, about 8 to 10 minutes. Drain on paper towels.

To make sandwich, arrange bottom part of rolls in a row, coat with mayonnaise and start to build your sandwich:

1) layer of sautéed onions
2) layer of mozzarella cheese
3) chicken breast
4) sprinkle generously with Parmesan cheese
5) repeat with layers of onions, mozzarella cheese and finish with sliced tomatoes
6) sprinkle with seasoned salt.

Top the sandwich and slice in half. Serve with black olives and fresh pickle sticks. For added zest, lightly spread Dijon mustard on each side of roll.

Yields 4 servings.

Wine selection: Sebaste Arneis, a dry white

Razorback Omelet

¹/₂ cup ham, diced
¹/₂ cup chicken, diced
¹/₄ cup vegetable oil
1 large potato, peeled and diced
2 pimentos, minced
2 medium onions, peeled and minced
¹/₂ cup canned tomatoes
salt and pepper to taste
¹/₂ teaspoon oregano
2 tablespoons parsley
10 eggs, beaten

Add oil and preheat electric skillet to 350°. Brown potatoes, onions and parsley, turning frequently until soft. Add ham, chicken, tomatoes, oregano and pimentos; salt and pepper. Cover and cook 5 minutes. Add 1 tablespoon water and 1 tablespoon milk to eggs and beat until well blended. Reduce heat on electric skillet to 310°. Add beaten eggs to mixture, cover and cook 6 minutes for a soft omelet or 10 minutes for a well-done omelet. Remove cover and let cool 2 or 3 minutes. Slice into wedges and serve with your favorite hot bread.

Yields 10 to 12 servings.

Wine selection: Korbel Brut, dry, sparkling

Sunday Egg Brunch

10 hard-boiled eggs
4 large tomatoes, sliced
1 cup buttered bread crumbs

Cheese sauce:

2 cups milk
4 tablespoons flour
4 tablespoons margarine
1 1/2 cups American cheese, grated or cubed

Melt butter in saucepan, then add flour, stirring until mixture becomes foamy, but not brown. Add milk slowly, stirring constantly to insure smoothness. Cook until thickened. Salt and pepper to taste. Blend in cheese over very low heat until it melts. One teaspoon Worcestershire sauce may be added.

Cut eggs in half and place in greased casserole dish. Cover each egg with a tomato slice. Salt and pepper to taste. Pour cheese sauce over tomatoes and sprinkle with buttered bread crumbs. Bake in 400° oven until brown on top, about 15 to 20 minutes. Serve on toasted English muffin or toast.

Yields 6 to 8 servings.

Wine selection: Kendall Jackson Johannisberg Riesling, a medium-bodied sweet white

Veggie Egg Omelet Deluxe

9 large eggs, beaten
²/₃ teaspoon salt
¹/₃ teaspoon black pepper
2 tablespoons water
2 tablespoons cream or milk
2 teaspoons parsley, finely minced
¹/₂ cup cheddar cheese, shredded
4 fresh green onions, chopped, include ²/₃ of tails
1 large tomato, cut up in small pieces
6 slices bacon, diced

Brown bacon and green onions in heavy skillet. Drain most of grease off and save. Add tomatoes and mix thoroughly. Salt and pepper to taste and cover. Cook over low heat 5 minutes, stirring occasionally. Combine eggs, salt, pepper, water, milk or cream, parsley and cheese; blend thoroughly. In an electric skillet, add 2 tablespoons bacon drippings. Preheat oven to 325°. Combine bacon, tomato and onion. Mix with egg mixture and pour into skillet. Cover tightly and cook 6 minutes for a soft omelet or 8 minutes for a firm omelet. Turn heat off and let cool 5 minutes. Serve with hot biscuits or toast.

or

In a 9-inch baking dish, add 2 tablespoons bacon drippings. Add egg mixture and stir in the bacon, tomato and onion mix. Place in preheated oven at 400° 12 to 14 minutes. Remove and cool 5 minutes.

Yields 6 to 8 servings.

Eggs and Veggie Frittata

1 pound ricotta
1 cup Parmesan cheese
1 medium zucchini, cubed
1 10-ounce package frozen spinach, thawed or 1 pound fresh
4 large eggs, beaten
1/4 cup fresh parsley, chopped coarse
1 teaspoon garlic powder or 3 cloves, minced
salt and pepper to taste

Preheat oven to 375°. In a large mixing bowl, combine all ingredients and mix. Spray a medium-size pan with Pam and pour mixture into it. Bake 30 minutes or until bubbly. Let cool 10 minutes before serving. Serve on toasted English muffins and garnish with thinly sliced sweet red onions.

Yields 8 servings.

Eggs Primavera

6 large eggs, beaten
2 medium zucchini squash, cut in half lengthwise and sliced in thin rounds
2 bunches green onions, cut in 1-inch pieces, including some tails
1/2 pound cherry tomatoes, cut in half
1 1/2 cups mushrooms, sliced thin
1/2 cup fresh green peas or frozen, thawed
3 tablespoons pure olive oil
salt and pepper to taste

In a large non-stick skillet, sauté vegetables in olive oil 8 to 9 minutes. Lower heat to medium. Add eggs and stir in vegetables until completely coated. Cover and cook until eggs set to desired consistency. Serve on dry toast for a low cal brunch.

Yields 6 servings.

Wine selection: Charles Shaw Napa Gamay, a fruity, soft, light-bodied dry red

Chick'N Egg Brunch

3 cups cooked chicken or turkey, diced
6 slices bacon
1 medium onion, chopped
1/3 cup green Spanish olives, chopped
2 tablespoons pimento, chopped
1 small can mushrooms, drained and cut into pieces or 1 cup fresh
2 tablespoons milk or cream
4 eggs

Cut bacon into small pieces and fry until crisp. Remove pieces from pan and sauté chopped onions and mushrooms in bacon fat until tender. Stir in cooked chicken, bacon, green olives and pimento and cook 5 minutes over medium heat. Beat eggs and milk together and add to chicken mixture, stirring continuously until of medium to firm consistency. Salt and pepper to taste. Serve on toasted buns as Sloppy Joes or on a toasted English muffin along with a peach and cottage cheese salad or your favorite Jello salad.

Yields 6 to 8 servings.

All American Eggs Frittata

8 large eggs
1 pound frozen or fresh hashed potatoes
3/4 pound whole hog pork sausage, browned and drained
1 large tomato, sliced in 7 slices 1/4-inch thick
1 green bell pepper, sliced in 7 slices 1/4-inch thick
salt and pepper to taste
1 large yellow onion, sliced thin
1 cup mushrooms, sliced
3/4 cup fresh or frozen green peas
1/4 cup fresh parsley, chopped
1/2 pound mozzarella cheese, cut in 1/4-inch cubes
1/3 cup Parmesan cheese, grated

In a non-stick 10-inch omelet frying pan, brown sausage; remove with a slotted spoon on paper towels. Over medium heat sauté peas, mushrooms and onions 6 to 7 minutes. Remove and drain on paper towels. Wipe pan clean (do not wash); line with potatoes on bottom and sides. Salt and pepper to taste. Blend eggs; add parsley, sausage, sautéed vegetables and cheeses and gently mix. Place pan over medium heat and pour egg mixture over potatoes. When eggs begin to set, run spatula around edge allowing eggs to run down the sides, one time only. Arrange sliced tomatoes on top of eggs and a slice of pepper on each slice of tomato. Salt and pepper to taste and cover tightly. Cook over low heat 7 minutes. Turn off heat. Let stand covered 7 minutes before serving.

Yields 6 to 8 servings.

Wine selection: Chenin Blanc or Johannisberg Riesling

Eggs Messina

3 cups frozen hash brown potatoes
6 slices of bacon, cut in 1-inch pieces
1 medium onion, chopped
4 to 6 green onions with tails, chopped
2 medium tomatoes, chopped
4 to 6 large eggs
salt and pepper to taste

In an electric skillet at 325° or heavy skillet over medium heat, brown bacon until crisp. Add potatoes and onions and brown 5 minutes. Add tomatoes, salt and pepper to taste, cover and cook 5 minutes. Break 4 to 6 eggs on top of mixture, salt and pepper to taste, cover and cook 4 to 5 minutes or longer if you want the eggs well-done.

Yields 4 to 6 servings.

Fettuccine Romano

1 pound fettuccine, cooked al dente

Sauce:

1 cup heavy whipping cream
3 cloves garlic, minced or 1 teaspoon garlic powder
4 ounces unsalted butter
1/2 cup Parmesan cheese, grated

In a heavy saucepan melt butter. Add cream, garlic and cheese. Stir and slowly heat to medium-hot, do not boil. Add immediately to cooked fettuccine; toss and serve on warm plates.

Variations:

2 tablespoons fresh parsley, coarsely chopped

1/2 pound small shrimp, sautéed 6 minutes in olive oil

3 flats of anchovies, chopped fine

Yields 6 servings.

Wine selection: Robert Mondavi Fume Blanc Reserve

Baked Lasagna

1 pound lasagna, cooked exactly 9 minutes in 6 quarts of salted water
8 ounces mozzarella cheese, shredded
1 cup Parmesan cheese, grated
1 pound ricotta cheese, blend in 2 large eggs
Prepare *Forty-five Minute Meat Sauce*

Cool lasagna and drain on paper towels. Preheat oven to 375°. Cover bottom of a 12 × 9 × 2-inch baking pan with meat sauce. Lay 4 lasagna noodles on top of sauce, slightly overlapping. Spread ¼ of the ricotta cheese mix over noodles. Cover cheese with ½ cup of sauce and sprinkle with mozzarella and Parmesan cheese. Repeat to make 3 layers; cover with Parmesan cheese. Bake uncovered 40 minutes. Let cool 5 minutes.

Wine selection: Simi Cabernet Sauvignon or Bertani Valpolicella, medium-bodied dry reds

Veggie Lasagna

1 pound lasagna, cooked 9 minutes in 6 quarts salted water
8 ounces mozzarella cheese, shredded
1¼ cup Parmesan cheese, shredded
1 pound ricotta, blended with 2 large eggs
salt and pepper to taste
¼ cup fresh parsley, chopped fine
Fresh Tomato Sauce I
2 zucchini or 1 large eggplant, cut in ¼-inch rounds and seasoned

Cool noodles and drain on paper towels. Lightly brown zucchini or eggplant in vegetable oil over medium-high heat. Drain on paper towels. Sprinkle with Parmesan cheese. Preheat oven to 375°. Cover bottom of a 9 × 12 × 2-inch lasagna pan with layer of tomato sauce. Arrange 4 noodles on top of sauce, slightly overlapping. Make layers of ricotta mix, tomato sauce, mozzarella and Parmesan cheese and zucchini or eggplant. Bake uncovered 40 minutes. Remove from oven and cool 10 minutes.

Yields 12 to 15 servings.

Wine selection: Ruffino Chianti Classico or Antinori Orvietto Classico

Pasta Al Furno

1 pound ziti or small rigatoni or mostaccioli, cooked 9 minutes in 6 quarts salted water
Forty-five Minute Meat Sauce, add 1½ cups water 10 minutes before finished cooking

Cheese blend:

1 pound ricotta
½ pound mozzarella cheese, shredded
½ cup Parmesan cheese, grated
⅔ teaspoon pepper
2 tablespoons fresh parsley, chopped coarse

Preheat oven to 375°. Mix all ingredients and blend in 5 cups tomato sauce. Mix should be semi-thick—add ½ cup water if needed and blend again. Cover the bottom of a 9 × 12 × 2-inch baking pan with cheese and cover with layers of sauce and pasta. Bake 40 minutes. Serve with Parmesan cheese.

Yields 10 to 12 servings.

Wine selection: Brolio Chianti Classico or Robert Mondavi Red

Stuffed Manicotti

1 box manicotti, cooked in 6 quarts salted water 10 minutes
Quickie Twenty Minute Sauce

Cheese filling:

$^1/_2$ cup mozzarella cheese, shredded
$^1/_2$ cup Parmesan cheese, grated
1 pound ricotta
2 large eggs, beaten
2 tablespoons parsley, chopped coarse
1 teaspoon garlic powder
$^1/_2$ teaspoon pepper

Meat filling:

1 pound lean ground beef or $^1/_2$ pork + $^1/_2$ beef or chicken or turkey
1 large egg
2 slices bread, soaked in water, lightly squeeze out excess water
1 teaspoon salt
$^1/_2$ teaspoon pepper
1 teaspoon garlic powder
2 tablespoons parsley, chopped coarse

Drain pasta and add cold water until lukewarm; leave in water until ready to stuff. Stuff manicotti with your favorite filling loosely, but full. Cover bottom of baking dish with sauce and stuffed manicotti in rows. Sprinkle with Romano or Parmesan cheese and bake in a preheated 375° oven 30 minutes (cheese) or 40 minutes (beef).

Wine selection:

With cheese—Fazi Battaglia Verdicchio

With meat—Besano Barlo or California Sebastini Pinot Noir

Eggplant Parmigiana

2 large eggplants, peeled and cut in ¼-inch rounds
Quickie Twenty Minute Sauce
4 ounces mozzarella cheese, shredded
½ cup Parmesan cheese, grated
olive oil, extra virgin or pure

Soak eggplant in salted water 1 hour, drain on paper towels, brown lightly in olive oil and drain again. Preheat oven to 350°. In a 10 × 10 × 2-inch casserole dish, cover bottom with tomato sauce. Make layers of browned eggplant, tomato sauce and mozzarella and Parmesan cheese. Bake 30 minutes.

Yields 6 to 8 servings.

Wine selection: Gallo Cabernet Sauvignon

Messina Chicken Eggplant Parmagian

4 3-ounce boneless, skinless chicken fillets or veal cutlets
8 slices eggplant, peeled
4 ounces mozzarella cheese, shredded
4 ounces Parmesan cheese, grated
½ cup pure olive oil
salt and pepper to taste

Breading:
⅔ cup dry bread crumbs
⅓ cup Parmesan cheese, grated
1 teaspoon garlic powder
2 tablespoons parsley, chopped coarse

Preheat oven to 400°. Using a wooden mallet, gently pound each piece of meat to tenderize. Salt and pepper to taste; set aside. Place eggplant on paper towels and sprinkle with salt. Let stand ½ hour. Pat dry and sauté in oil until lightly browned on each side. Drain on paper towels. Dip chicken or veal in olive oil and coat with breading; set aside. Brush bottom of baking pan with oil. Make layers of eggplant, chicken or veal, tomato sauce and cheeses. Bake 25 minutes. Serve with fettuccine.

Yields 4 servings.

Wine selection: Glen Ellen Cabernet Sauvignon

Rice and Italian Sausage

1 pound Italian sausage, cut in 1-inch pieces
4 cups chicken broth, fresh or canned
2 large tomatoes, chopped coarse
1 large yellow onion, sliced thin
1 cup mushrooms, sliced
1 large bell pepper, cut in 1/4-inch slices
3 cloves garlic, chopped fine
2 tablespoons olive oil, extra virgin or pure
3/4 cup long grain rice
salt and pepper to taste

In a 4-quart pot, brown sausage in olive oil. Remove and drain on paper towels. Sauté onions until lightly brown. Add mushrooms and pepper and sauté 2 or 3 minutes. Add sausage and remaining ingredients except rice and bring to a boil. Add rice and cook until tender, about 18 minutes. Serve with Italian bread.

Yields 6 servings.

Wine selection: California Beringer Fume Blanc

Italian Sausage

4 1/2- to 5-pounds pork shoulder, boned and cut in 1/2-inch pieces
4 tablespoons fennel seed
2 tablespoons salt
1 tablespoon black pepper, coarse ground
1 teaspoon flaked red pepper (more if desired)
1 teaspoon garlic powder
1/4 cup fresh parsley, chopped fine
Natural pork casings (can be obtained at specialty butcher shop)

On a clean surface, spread pork meat out evenly. Sprinkle all the ingredients on meat. Blend using hands to ensure even coating. Set up grinder with stuffing attachment. Grind and stuff into casings. If casings not available, make into patties. Can be grilled, fried or cooked in tomato sauce. Remainder should be placed in ZipLoc bag and frozen for future use (no longer than 6 weeks).

Polenta/Italian Sausage and Peppers

1¹/₂ cups yellow cornmeal
2 teaspoons salt
Sausage and Peppers Sauce

In a 4-quart sauce pan, bring salted water to a boil. Slowly add cornmeal, stirring constantly until all the corn meal has been added. Reduce heat and simmer 25 to 30 minutes. Stir frequently. Polenta should be very thick. Pour onto a large serving platter and let set about 10 minutes. Cut in 2-inch squares and pour **Sausage and Peppers Sauce** *over polenta.*

Sausage and Peppers Sauce

Make **Quickie Twenty Minute Sauce***. Cut 1¹/₂ pounds of Italian sausage in bite-size pieces and simmer in sauce 30 minutes. Add 2 green peppers cut in strips and simmer an additional 10 minutes. Let stand 10 minutes.*

Yields 6 servings.

Wine selection: Foppiano Petite Sirah, a robust dry red

Tripe Al Modo Siciliano

2 pounds beef tripe (honeycomb preferred)
1 large yellow onion, sliced thin
2 medium carrots, sliced in ¹/₄-inch pieces
1 cup celery, cut in ¹/₂-inch pieces, include leaves
2 large tomatoes, chopped coarse
1 16-ounce can tomato sauce
3 large cloves garlic, minced
salt and pepper to taste
1 teaspoon flaked red pepper or to taste
1 tablespoon oregano
¹/₂ cup fresh parsley, chopped coarse
¹/₄ cup olive oil, extra virgin or pure
1 large meaty bell pepper, cored and cut in ¹/₂-inch strips
1 pound linguine, cooked

Boil tripe in salted water 1 hour. Cool under running water. Trim all excess fat. Cut in bite-size pieces; set aside. Lightly sauté onions, garlic, celery and parsley in olive oil 6 to 7 minutes. Add remaining ingredients except bell pepper and simmer 5 minutes. Adjust seasoning, add tripe, cover and simmer 40 minutes. Add bell pepper, stir, cover and simmer an additional 15 minutes. Serve over linguine.

Yields 6 servings.

Wine selection: Barolo-Red Bersano

Fried/Broiled Beef Tripe

1 24-ounce can beef tripe (Armour) or 2- to 2½-pounds fresh, cut in 2 × 3-inch pieces
1 large egg, beaten and mixed with ½ cup milk
1 cup flour, seasoned or self-rising corn meal
½ cup pure olive oil or more if needed

Breading:

⅔ cup dry bread crumbs
⅓ cup Parmesan cheese
1 teaspoon garlic powder

Cooking fresh tripe:

Place tripe in pot with 4 quarts water, 1 tablespoon salt, 2 bay leaves and 1 stalk celery. Cook 1½ hours. Cool and cut in 2 × 3-inch pieces.

To fry tripe:

Place flour on a flat surface. Coat tripe in egg-milk mix and roll in flour. Shake off excess. Fry in oil until golden brown on each side. Drain on paper towels.

To broil tripe:

Preheat broiler to 500°. Dip tripe in olive oil and coat with bread crumbs. Line broiler pan with foil and place 4 to 5 inches from heat. Broil tripe about 3 to 4 minutes on each side or until golden brown. Remove and place on a warm serving platter.

Yields 6 servings.

Wine selection: Gancia Brut Spumanti or Banfi Brut Spumanti

Hungarian Paprika Tripe

4 pounds beef honeycomb tripe
1 large onion, sliced thin
2 tablespoons paprika
salt and pepper to taste
3 tomatoes, cut in bite-size pieces
1 large bell pepper, cut in thin strips
olive oil

Clean tripe, boil in salted water 1 hour, drain, cool and cut into bite-size pieces. In a large skillet, sauté onions in olive oil. Lower heat and stir in paprika. Add tripe, season with salt and pepper and sauté 20 minutes. Add $^1/_4$ cup water and continue cooking, adding small amounts of water as needed. Stir occasionally and cook 40 minutes. Add tomatoes and pepper, stir, cover and cook 15 minutes. Serve with boiled potatoes and cabbage.

Yields 6 servings.

Wine selection: J. Lohr Monterey Gamay, a light to medium-bodied red

Samulichiu I
Basting Sauce for Broiling and Baking

$^1/_4$ cup red wine vinegar
2 tablespoons lemon juice
2 cloves garlic, crushed
$1^1/_2$ teaspoons oregano
salt and pepper to taste
2 tablespoons fresh parsley
$^1/_2$ cup water
$^1/_4$ cup olive oil, extra virgin or pure

Blend thoroughly. Use for basting chicken while broiling or when baking a whole chicken. Can be kept in a covered jar for several weeks.

Sicilian Basting Sauce II

For Chicken and Turkey

¹/₄ cup red wine vinegar
¹/₃ cup olive oil, extra virgin or pure
¹/₂ cup water
2 tablespoons lemon juice
3 cloves garlic
1 tablespoon oregano
1 teaspoon salt
1 teaspoon black pepper
¹/₂ teaspoon red flaked pepper
2 tablespoons fresh parsley, minced
2 tablespoons fresh basil, minced or 2 teaspoons dry

Blend all ingredients thoroughly in a blender 2 minutes. Stir each time before using for basting chickens on the grill. Can also be used for broiling or baking chickens in the oven.

Desserts

Italian dolce are famous for their tantalizing combination of full flavor and creamy texture. Expresso is the perfect finishing touch, along with wines and cordials. Italy produces a variety of after dinner drinks that fit any palate and are a perfect finale for your Sicilian dinner.

Wines:

Martini and Rossi Asti Spumanti, a delightful sparkling wine

Lungarotti Vin Santo, slightly sweet

Reccioti della Soave Anselmi, light and fruity

Marsala, a soft, sweet, medium-bodied red

Cordials:

Amaretto

Strega

Galliano

Sambucco

Cynar

Frangelico

Sicilian Fruit Dessert

2 cups honeydew melon balls
1 cup navel orange sections, bite-size
1 cup Bosc pears, bite-size
1 cup Bartlet or D'ageu pears, bite-size
1 cup apple, bite-size
½ cup each of white, red and black grapes
3 tablespoons sugar
2 ounces grenadine

Blend all ingredients together in a mixing bowl. Refrigerate several hours. Serve chilled. Use as a dessert or first course.

Yields 15 to 20 servings.

Sicilian Peach Cooler

3 ripe peaches, peeled and quartered
3 rounded tablespoons sugar or honey
6 ounces dry white wine

Place all ingredients in a blender set at medium speed for 1 minute. Chill and serve as a cool dessert or over ice cream. May add 1 ounce of your favorite liqueur.

Peaches and Pears/Wine

1 pound peaches, peeled and sliced
1 pound pears, peeled and sliced
1 1/2 cups dry white wine
1/2 cup sugar or honey
1 ounce of your favorite liqueur (optional)

In a large mixing bowl, combine wine, sugar or honey and liqueur. Add peaches and pears and gently toss. Place in refrigerator overnight. Serve chilled as dessert or appetizer.

Variations:

Fill wine glass 3/4 full with peach slices, then add a dry red wine. Chill several hours. (Recipe can be put in blender 1 minute at medium speed and used for topping on cakes.)

Yields 8 to 10 servings.

Sicilian Cannoli/Ricotta Filling

Filling:
1 pound ricotta cheese
3/4 cup powdered sugar
1 teaspoon pure vanilla
1/4 cup heavy whipping cream
1/3 cup mixed candied fruit, chopped medium
2 tablespoons semisweet chocolate chips

Blend ricotta, cream and sugar until smooth. Stir in candied fruit and chocolate chips. Chill until ready to fill shells.

Fills 10 cannoli shells.

Cannoli Shells

3 cups all-purpose flour
1/4 cup sugar
1 teaspoon cinnamon
1/4 teaspoon salt
4 tablespoons vegetable shortening
1 large egg, slightly beaten
1/4 cup sweet vermouth or port wine

Mix sugar, flour, cinnamon and salt. Cut in shortening, add egg and blend. Add wine and mix until smooth. Turn on a floured surface and knead 10 minutes. Cover and refrigerate 3 hours or overnight.

Making Cannoli shells with pasta machine:

Set on #8 roller opening. Run 1/3 dough through rollers 2 to 3 times, lightly flour if needed. Dough should be at least 5 inches wide. Set machine on #6, flour lightly and roll out dough. Set on #5 and roll out final time. Lay dough on floured surface and cut out 5-inch diameter circles. Roll loosely on aluminum cannoli tubes. Bake on cookie sheet at 475° 12 to 14 minutes or until lightly browned.
(If you don't have a pasta machine, roll dough by hand to less than 1/8-inch thickness.)

To fry:

Place in a preheated deep fryer with 4 inches vegetable oil at 360° and fry shells 1 minute or until golden brown. Drain on paper towels. When cool, remove shells from tubes carefully and chill. Use a pastry bag to fill shells. Dip each end in chopped pistachio nuts. Place on serving tray and sprinkle with powdered sugar. Chill. This recipe makes about 20 shells. Extra shells may be frozen for later use.

Fresh Fruit Sorbet

1 pound peaches, peeled and pitted

1 pound apples, peeled and cored

1 pound pears, peeled and cored

2 cups watermelon

1 cup canteloupe

1 cup sugar

juice of 1 lemon

1 cup orange juice

Cube fruit and place in food processor 1 minute at medium speed. Add sugar, lemon juice and orange juice. Blend 1 minute. Pour into large mold and freeze. Serve with your favorite cookies or cake.

Yields 20 servings.

Sicilian Biscotta

Blend all dry ingredients:

5 pounds all-purpose flour

2 pounds granulated sugar

1 tablespoon salt

$1/2$ cup double action baking powder

2 tablespoons cinnamon

Blend all liquid ingredients:

12 large eggs, reserve 2 whites

$1/2$ quart whole milk

$1/2$ pound butter, melted

$1 1/2$ tablespoons pure vanilla extract

Place flour mixture on large counter top. Make large hole in middle. Pour egg mixture into hole. Slowly, with your fingers, blend the liquids into the dry flour mixture. Work the mixture until you have a moist loaf. If it sticks, sprinkle flour on counter and work until pliable (10 to 15 minutes). Place in bowl and cover. Preheat oven to 375°. Tear small pieces off and roll on a floured surface about size of your middle finger. Cut into 6- to 7-inch pieces and form into rings. Place on cookie sheets $1/2$ inch apart. Beat egg whites and brush on rings before baking. Bake about 25 to 30 minutes or until golden brown. After all the biscotta are baked reduce oven heat to 200°. Place all the biscotta on the cookie sheets and place in oven 2 hours. Turn heat off and leave overnight. Place biscotta in a large covered container. They will stay fresh for months.

Ricotta Pie

1 9-inch pie crust
2 pounds ricotta cheese
1 cup sugar
4 tablespoons honey
1 tablespoon flour
2 teaspoons pure vanilla extract
1/2 teaspoon cinnamon
1/4 teaspoon nutmeg
2 large eggs
1 teaspoon each orange and lemon peel, grated
2 tablespoons mixed candied fruit, chopped
2 tablespoons pine nuts or walnuts

Preheat oven to 350°. Combine all dry ingredients. Combine all liquid ingredients including eggs and blend. Place ricotta in a large mixing bowl. Blend in the liquids. Then slowly blend in the dry mix. Continue beating until thoroughly blended and smooth. Arrange pie crust in a 9-inch pan and pour in cheese mixture. Sprinkle pine nuts evenly on top. Bake in middle of oven 40 minutes. Pie should be firm. Cool, then chill 2 hours and serve.

Italian Cheese Cake

1 pound ricotta cheese, room temperature
1 pound cream cheese, room temperature
1 pound sour cream
1 1/2 cups sugar
4 large eggs, slightly beaten
1 teaspoon fresh lemon juice
1 teaspoon lemon rind, grated
1 tablespoon pure vanilla
1 stick butter, melted

Mix together:

3 tablespoons flour
3 tablespoons corn starch

Do not preheat oven. Important to add ingredients as instructed. Blend ricotta and cream cheese. Gradually add sugar and blend. Stir in lemon rind and juice, vanilla and flour mix. Add butter and blend well by hand. Add sour cream and eggs and mix by hand. Spray 9-inch spring form pan with Pam. Fill with mix, place pan on cookie sheet and set the pan on a flat surface several times to remove air bubbles. Bake at 325° 1 1/2 hours. Do not open oven door. Turn off heat and leave cake in oven 2 hours.

Sicilian Casata

2 14- to 16-ounce pound cakes
1 can chocolate icing
1 pound ricotta cheese
2 tablespoons heavy cream
1/3 cup sugar
3 tablespoons candied fruit, chopped medium
2 ounces semisweet chocolate bits
rind of 1 orange and juice, grated
2 tablespoons Frangelica liqueur
1/3 cup pine nuts or chopped walnuts

Blend cheese, cream, sugar, orange rind and juice and liqueur. Stir in chocolate bits or candied fruit. Set aside. Cut pound cakes horizontally into 3 layers.

To assemble:

Place bottom layer on a cake dish. Cover evenly with 1/4 ricotta mix. Cover with second piece of pound cake and cover with 1/4 ricotta mix. Top with third piece of cake. Cover with chocolate icing. Sprinkle nuts on top and decorate with 4 or 5 maraschino cherries. Refrigerate overnight and serve chilled.

Fraviolli

1 pound ricotta
4 tablespoons honey
³/₄ teaspoon cinnamon or 1 teaspoon pure vanilla
¹/₂ cup granulated sugar

Dough:

4 cups all-purpose flour
1 teaspoon baking powder
¹/₂ teaspoon salt
4 rounded tablespoons shortening
1¹/₃ cups milk

Mix flour, salt and baking powder. Blend in shortening. Add milk and mix. On a lightly floured board, roll out dough to ¹/₈-inch thick. Use coffee saucer to cut out pie shapes. Place 1¹/₂ tablespoons cheese mix in center of pie dough. Fold over and use fork to seal. Fry in ¹/₂-inch vegetable oil on medium-high heat. Fry 3 to 4 minutes on each side, then drain on paper towels. Sprinkle with granulated sugar and let cool before serving.

Yields 16 to 18 pies.

Egg Custard for the Rich and Famous

10 large egg yolks
5 cups heavy whipping cream
2 teaspoons pure vanilla extract
¹/₄ teaspoon salt
1 cup sugar
²/₃ cup light brown sugar

Preheat oven to 300°. Blend cream, vanilla and salt in a heavy saucepan and heat, do not boil, 5 to 6 minutes. Combine egg yolks and sugars. Slowly dribble the hot cream mix into the egg yolk mix, stirring constantly. In a large roasting pan, arrange 8 to 9 1-cup-size ramekins. Pour egg and cream mix in a pitcher. Fill ramekins ¹/₂ inch from top. Place roasting pan in oven and add hot water to pan halfway up the ramekins. Cover loosely with foil and bake 1¹/₄ hours. Check during last 10 minutes. If custard is firm around edges, remove from oven. Place ramekins on counter to cool. Refrigerate several hours and serve.

Variations:

Add ¹/₄ cup Amaretto liqueur.

Add ¹/₄ cup Frangelico liqueur.

Add ¹/₄ cup Truffles du chocolat liqueur.

Rice Pudding for the Rich and Famous

4 cups cooked rice
1 quart heavy cream
1 tablespoon cornstarch
12 large egg yolks
1 teaspoon lemon rind
2 teaspoons lemon juice
1 1/4 cups sugar
1/4 cup Amaretto liqueur

Preheat oven to 325°. Place large pan of hot water on lower rack. In a large mixing bowl, cream egg yolks, sugar and cornstarch. Add cream and remaining ingredients. Blend. Pour into a 9 × 12 × 2-inch baking pan and place on rack over pan of water. Bake 30 minutes or until pudding begins to thicken; gently stir so that rice is evenly distributed. Continue baking 40 minutes. Cool, then refrigerate 2 hours. Serve chilled.

Yields 15 servings.

Don's Zuppa Inglese

1 12- to 14-ounce pound cake, cut in 1/4-inch slices

Cream filling:

3 egg yolks
3 ounces powdered sugar
5 tablespoons flour
2 cups milk or half-and-half, heated 200°
1 teaspoon lemon rind, grated

Combine eggs and sugar. Mix thoroughly. Add flour 1 tablespoon at a time and blend. Add hot milk slowly and mix. Place in double boiler and thicken. Cool and add lemon rind.

Chocolate filling:

2 ounces semisweet chocolate, melted
4 ounces blackberry flavored brandy or 4 ounces rum

Layer with 1 slice of cake, brandy or rum, cream filling and then chocolate. Alternate until all ingredients are used. Save enough cream filling to cover top. The dessert should be in the shape of an elongated dome. Garnish with candied cherries. Serve on a bed of raspberry or strawberry sauce.

Yields 8 to 10 servings.

Egg Custard for Everyday

6 large eggs
2 cups half-and-half
$^1/_2$ cup sugar
$^1/_2$ cup light brown sugar
$^1/_4$ stick butter, melted
pinch of salt
1 teaspoon pure vanilla extract

*Preheat oven to 350°. Combine all ingredients and blend. Pour egg mixture into a
6 × 10 × 2-inch oven proof dish and bake 30 minutes. Cool and refrigerate several hours
and serve chilled.*

Yields 6 to 8 servings.

Appendices

Cooking Terms

Boil—Cooking in water or liquid at boiling temperature. Bubbles will rise continually and break on the surface.

Broil—Cooking uncovered by direct heat, placing rack under the source of heat.

Pan-Broil—Cooking in lightly greased pan on top of stove. Pour fat off as it accumulates so food does not fry.

Baste—Moistening food while cooking by pouring melted fat, drippings or other liquid over it.

Cream—Mashing or mixing foods together until creamy.

Pan-Fry—Cooking in small amount of fat in fry pan.

Knead—Pressing, stretching and folding dough mixture to make it smooth. Bread dough will become elastic.

Parboil—Boiling until partly cooked.

Scald—Heating liquid to just below boiling point.

Simmer—Cooking in liquid just below boiling point. Bubbles will form slowly and break below surface.

Stew—Boiling or simmering in small amount of liquid.

Braise—Cooking slowly in fat and little moisture in closed pot.

Substitutions for a Missing Ingredient

1 square chocolate (1 ounce) = 3 or 4 tablespoons cocoa plus ½ tablespoon fat.

1 tablespoon cornstarch (for thickening) = 2 tablespoons flour.

1 cup sifted all-purpose flour = 1 cup plus 2 tablespoons sifted cake flour.

1 cup sifted cake flour = 1 cup minus 2 tablespoons sifted all-purpose flour.

1 teaspoon baking powder = ¼ teaspoon baking soda plus ½ teaspoon cream of tartar.

1 cup sour milk = 1 cup sweet milk into which 1 tablespoon vinegar or lemon juice has been stirred; or 1 cup buttermilk (let stand for 5 minutes).

1 cup sweet milk = 1 cup sour milk or buttermilk plus ½ teaspoon baking soda.

¾ cup cracker crumbs = 1 cup bread crumbs.

1 cup cream, sour, heavy = ⅓ cup butter and ⅔ cup milk in any sour milk recipe.

1 teaspoon dried herbs = 1 tablespoon fresh herbs.

1 cup whole milk = ½ cup evaporated milk and ½ cup water or

1 cup reconstituted nonfat dry milk and 1 tablespoon butter.

1 package active dry yeast = 1 cake compressed yeast.

1 tablespoon instant minced onion, rehydrated = 1 small fresh onion.

1 tablespoon prepared mustard = 1 teaspoon dry mustard.

⅓ teaspoon garlic powder = 1 large pressed clove of garlic.

1 pound whole dates = 1½ cups pitted and cut.

3 medium bananas = 1 cup mashed.

3 cups dry corn flakes = 1 cup crushed.

10 miniature marshmallows = 1 large marshmallow.

Herb Guide

Basil—potatoes, cheese, eggs, fish, lamb, tomatoes, peas, squash, duck

Bay Leaf—soups, meat, stews, tomato sauces and juice

Chervil—chicken, peas, egg and cheese dishes, spinach, green salads

Chives—eggs, potatoes, salads, garnish for meat and fish

Dill—fish, potatoes, pickles, tomatoes, cream and cottage cheese, fish and vegetable salads

Garlic—meats, vegetables, salads, egg, cheese

Marjoram—vegetable soups, eggs, cheese dishes, beef, lamb, stuffings

Mint—beverages, cakes, pies, ice cream, candies, jellies, potatoes

Oregano—tomato sauces, pizza, vegetable salads, chili, pork and veal

Parsley—meat, vegetables, eggs, cheese, soup

Rosemary—potatoes, cauliflower, fish, duck, veal, poultry stuffing

Sage—sausages, poultry, hamburgers, pork, stuffings

Savory—meat, eggs, salads, chicken, soups

Tarragon—vinegar, pickles, chicken, tomatoes, sauces for vegetables and meats, egg and cheese dishes, fish, salads

Thyme—soups, beef, lamb, veal, pork, oysters, fish, eggs, cheese, stuffings

Table of Equivalents

Standard Equivalents

A few grains . . . . .¹/₈ teaspoon
1 coffee spoon . . . . .¹/₄ teaspoon
60 drops . . . . .1 teaspoon
3 teaspoons . . . . .1 tablespoon
2 tablespoons . . . . .1 fluid ounce
16 fluid ounces . . . . .1 pint
16 ounces . . . . .1 pound
16 tablespoons. . . . . .1 cup
1 cup. . . . . .¹/₂ pint
2 pints. . . . . .1 quart
4 cups . . . . .1 quart
4 quarts. . . . . .1 gallon
8 quarts . . . . .1 peck
4 pecks . . . . .1 bushel

Nut Equivalents

Almonds

1 pound in shell . . . . .1 cup shelled
1 cup whole. . . . . .5¹/₂ ounces
1 cup grated . . . . .2¹/₂ ounces
1 cup chopped . . . . .4¹/₂ ounces
2¹/₂ cups ground . . . . .8 ounces
1 cup ground. . . . . .3¹/₂ ounces
1 cup blanched . . . . .1¹/₃ cup
1 cup blanched, ground. . . . . .1¹/₃ ounces
1 cup blanched. . . . . .1¹/₃ cups sliced

Coconut

1 cup dry shredded . . . . .2 ounces
1¹/₂ cup moist shredded. . . . . .4 ounces
3¹/₂ cups grated . . . . .8 ounces
5 cups fresh . . . . .1 pound

Peanuts

1 pound in shell. . . . . .¹/₂ pound shelled
1 cup meats. . . . . .1¹/₃ cup ground
1¹/₂ pound meats. . . . . .3 cups chopped

Pecans

1 cup meats . . . . .4 ounces
1 cup meats. . . . . .1 cup ground
1 cup meats. . . . . .1²/₃ cup grated

Walnuts

1 pound in shell . . . . .2 cups shelled
1 cup grated. . . . . .3¹/₂ ounces
1 cup ground. . . . . .6 ounces
1 cup chopped . . . . .4 ounces

Index